General Editors: Professor A.N. Jeffares (*University
of Stirling*) & Professor Suheil Bushrui (*American
University of Beirut*)

Richard Brinsley Sheridan

THE RIVALS

Notes by A.N. Jeffares

MA PH D (DUBLIN) MA D PHIL (OXFORD)
Professor of English, University of Stirling

LONGMAN
YORK PRESS

YORK PRESS
Immeuble Esseily, Place Riad Solh, Beirut

LONGMAN GROUP LIMITED
Longman House, Burnt Mill, Harlow,
Essex CM20 2JE, England
Associated companies, branches and representatives
throughout the world

First published 1981
Eighth impression 1995

ISBN 0-582-78272-4

Produced by Longman Singapore Publishers Pte Ltd
Printed in Singapore

A0I756

Contents

Part 1: Introduction   *page* 5
  Life of Sheridan   5
  The stage in Sheridan's day   10
  A note on the text   12

Part 2: Summaries   14
  A general summary   14
  Detailed summaries   17

Part 3: Commentary   47
  The characters   47
  Plot   58
  Speech   60
  Staging   60

Part 4: Hints for study   61
  Questions and specimen answers   62

Part 5: Suggestions for further reading   66

The author of these notes   67

Part 1

Introduction

Life of Sheridan

Richard Brinsley Sheridan came of a literary family. His grandfather, the Reverend Thomas Sheridan, a country clergyman and a good teacher, a doctor of divinity with a Rabelaisian wit, was a close friend of Jonathan Swift, Dean of St Patrick's Cathedral, Dublin—the two men exchanged humorous verses and shared elaborate literary jokes. His father, Thomas Sheridan (1719–88), was an actor, playing parts in Dublin and at Drury Lane in London before becoming manager of the Smock Alley Theatre in Dublin. After a riot which destroyed the theatre in 1754 he moved to London, writing on education, before trying to build up the theatre audiences again in Dublin in 1756. The building of a second theatre put paid to his hopes there; in two year's time he left for England, to teach elocution with great success as well as compiling a dictionary. His wife, Frances Sheridan (1724–66), was a novelist and dramatist.

Their son, Richard Brinsley, was born in Dublin in 1751, his parents' third child. At the age of three he was left in Dublin with relatives, but had another two years there with his parents when his father was trying to establish his fortunes in the Smock Alley Theatre the second time. He went to Samuel Whyte's excellent school in Dublin, where he was considered, according to his biographer, the Irish poet Thomas Moore (1779–1852), who also went to Whyte's School, to be 'a most impenetrable dunce'. In 1759 he went to London, and was sent to the famous school of Harrow in 1762 at the age of eleven. He was unhappy at school and felt neglected, for his father had moved the rest of the family to France, to avoid being arrested for bankruptcy, and to economise. As the son of an indigent actor, Richard felt despised at school, and he was short of money and clothes. His mother died in France in 1766 and Thomas Sheridan then returned to England, having managed to arrange his financial affairs in Dublin. In 1769 Richard was taken from Harrow and, as his schoolmaster put it, was 'upon the town'. He had a year in London learning fencing and riding and being educated by his father.

In 1770 the family moved to Bath in Somerset. The city was then at the peak of its fashionable reputation. It had been a spa in early Roman times, and its hot springs, strongly recommended by physicians, drew many visitors. It became a social resort in the eighteenth century, and, under the influence of Richard ('Beau') Nash (1674–1762), who became Master of Ceremonies in 1705, was known for its etiquette and elegance. Nash cleaned up the Pump Room, hired a band, and had an Assembly Room built; he autocratically enforced a code of polite behaviour and manners upon those who came to Bath, and generally made the town popular. It was beautified by elegant squares and classical buildings. New Assembly Rooms were built in 1771; there were public breakfasts, concerts, plays, balls, walks to be enjoyed, as well as cards to be played, scandal to be talked, and the waters to be drunk. There was an intense social life in this town, frequented—as Oliver Goldsmith (1732–74) put it in his delightful *Life of Richard Nash* (1762)—'by people of distinction'. Bath was Richard Brinsley Sheridan's university: he danced, he wrote later, with all the women at Bath, wrote sonnets and verses in praise of some, satires and lampoons upon others, and in a very short time became 'the established wit and fashion of the place'.

He also became a romantic hero. He ran away to France with Elizabeth Ann Linley, the daughter of a singing master. The girl, who sang superbly as well as being particularly beautiful, was being pestered by a married man called Mathews, and had asked Sheridan's sister and then Sheridan himself for help. When Elizabeth's father brought her back from the continent he realised that Sheridan had behaved honourably, Mathews dishonourably. Richard and Elizabeth concealed the fact that they had been married in France (they were minors, so the marriage would have been invalid). Two duels with Mathews ensued on Sheridan's return, and in the second one Sheridan was seriously wounded. Elizabeth was having a startling success as a singer, at Oxford and at Drury Lane in London, but, despite the efforts of both Mr Sheridan and Mr Linley to keep them apart, Sheridan and Elizabeth got married in 1773.

Sheridan had been entered at the Middle Temple in London with the idea of becoming a barrister (there are many legal images in *The Rivals*), but he refused to let Elizabeth sing professionally again, despite tempting offers and their urgent need for housekeeping money. She did, however, sing at parties given by friends or by themselves, and as a result they lived an intense social life. He wrote *The Rivals*, using his knowledge of life in Bath and turning his own romantic—and very nearly tragic—experiences there into light-hearted comedy.

The success of *The Rivals* in January 1775—after an initial set-back— was followed in March of the same year by a lively farce, *St Patrick's Day*, and in November by *The Duenna*, which ran for seventy-five days. This was a year of triumph. Sheridan's initial misgivings about the theatre, based on his father's unhappy experiences, vanished, and the possibility of succeeding David Garrick (1717–79) as manager of the

Drury Lane Theatre seemed highly attractive. By 1776 he had borrowed enough money to buy the theatre from Garrick, who wanted £70,000 for it—Garrick's partner did not want to sell his half, so Sheridan was responsible for £35,000, and he produced this by adding to his own borrowed £10,000 contributions from other shareholders: his friend Ewart Lindley and his father-in-law each providing £10,000 and a Dr Ford the remaining £5,000.

In 1776 Sheridan put on *A Trip to Scarborough*, which was a politer version of an earlier play, *The Relapse* (1696), by Sir John Vanbrugh (1664–1726). The following year he wrote his masterpiece *The School for Scandal*; it was first performed on 8 May, and was immediately popular. Following its success came that of *The Critic* which was produced in 1779, and marked the peak of Sheridan's achievement. He borrowed more money to buy the shares of Garrick's partner, and thus became the sole proprietor of the Drury Lane Theatre.

Audiences crowded in, money poured in, and Sheridan was naturally extravagant. He was only twenty-eight, and supremely successful in the roles of manager and playwright—he had written his plays in four years of brilliant achievement.* He was also enormously popular socially. His ambition, however, was not satisfied. He wanted to escape from the world of the theatre into what seemed the similar but vastly larger world of politics.

Sheridan managed to get himself elected as Member of Parliament for Stafford (it cost him over a thousand pounds) in 1780. He enjoyed speaking in the House of Commons; and he enjoyed perhaps even more being a member of Brooks's, an exclusive Whig club in London. To have been elected was a triumph for him, since actors were not then automatically accepted into society. Sheridan had a vast appetite for continuing social success, and now he moved in circles of great wealth and political power, using the theatre as his own source of income, gambling, drinking, flirting. He was careless in managing his financial affairs; he commanded credit easily; but behind his wit and charm he had a serious outlook on life. His attitude to the American War of Independence shows his own independence and common sense, for he thought the Americans were treated foolishly. When the Tory government fell in 1782 Sheridan was made Under-Secretary of State for Foreign affairs in Lord Rockingham's administration. This was an able government, containing Edmund Burke (1729–97), an Irishman and renowned political philosopher; Lord Shelburne (1737–1805); and Sheridan's friend Charles James Fox (1749–1806). When Fox resigned after Rockingham's death (both he and Lord Shelburne, who succeeded Rockingham, disliked each other cordially) Sheridan followed him. But

* His last play was *Pizarro* (1799), a dull adaptation of a prose tragedy from the German of August Friedrich Ferdinand von Kotzebue (1761–1819).

there followed a coalition with Lord North, and Sheridan became a Secretary to the Treasury—a most unsuitable post, it would seem, for someone so casual and inefficient with finances. This ministry fell, because Fox had decided to launch his India Bill. Burke had collected the facts, and the Whigs had decided to put the government of India into the hands of Commissioners. The Bill was carried in the Commons, but the opposition of the King and the Lords killed it and Fox was defeated in the ensuing election.

Sheridan's wife felt the great world of politics and fashion was destroying their marriage; she urged him in letters full of devotion to have a quiet home in the country. She had no illusions about his political life, distrusting his optimism, and trying to persuade him to get some financial reward for himself in return for the vast amount of work he put into his politics. He, however, was too proud to ask for money, although the theatre's finances were becoming decidedly disordered. Sheridan simply could not agree with Elizabeth's pleas—the brilliant company he kept, the applause of the political audience, drew him; he felt he had to maintain the prominent position he had attained in the social and political world of London.

His reputation was further strengthened by the speeches he made in the House of Commons, at Burke's instigation, against Warren Hastings. Burke described Sheridan's mind as 'seldom unemployed but then like all such great and vigorous minds it takes an eagle flight by itself and we can hardly bring it to rustle along the ground, with us birds of meaner wing, in coveys'. And so Sheridan spoke for five hours in a speech which was lavishly praised in all quarters. Even the Tory leader William Pitt (1759–1806), diametrically opposed to him in politics, who did not particularly like Sheridan personally, said 'an abler speech had, perhaps, never been delivered'. Sheridan subsequently managed to speak on four days when Warren Hastings was impeached in Westminster Hall in 1788, with even greater effect.

Meanwhile his marriage suffered. There had been many strains upon it. Elizabeth became ill after giving birth to a daughter, Mary, in March 1792, and died in July. By October Mary too was dead. At forty-one Sheridan was left alone with a son, Tom (born in the great year of Sheridan's success, 1775). 1792 was a year of troubles for him: the Drury Lane theatre became unsafe, and had to be pulled down.

Sheridan set to work and was able, amazingly, to raise £150,000 to rebuild the theatre. The years after Elizabeth's death were filled with drinking, betting and incurring debts. He decided to marry again, and his choice fell on a young girl, Esther Ogle, twenty-three years younger than himself. They had a son, Charles Brinsley, born in 1796.

In 1802 the funds of the Drury Lane Theatre were impounded by an order of the Court of Chancery, and though Sheridan appeared in court, to speak eloquently for two hours, he lost his case. He continued his headlong progress in pursuit of money to pay his debts. Fox, in power again, made him Treasurer of the Navy but without a seat in the Cabinet. The two men had drifted apart over the years, Sheridan being jealous of his independence and Fox liking younger, more adaptable admirers. Sheridan did, however, get a place for his son, Tom, in Ireland and he managed to gain a place for himself (that of Receiver-General of the Duchy of Cornwall) from the Prince Regent, with whom he had been on very friendly terms for many years. He was no longer able to boast of his independence; both he and his son had become 'place men'. After Fox's death in 1806 Sheridan was elected as member for Westminster but he was defeated in an election a year later. However he gained another seat (which was in the gift of the Prince Regent) in Parliament at Ilchester.

Then came the fire which completely destroyed the Drury Lane Theatre in February 1809. Sheridan faced his loss with characteristic courage, remarking, as he viewed the conflagration from the Piazza Coffee House nearby, 'a man may surely take a glass of wine by his own fireside'. The situation was desperate; the theatre had been worth over four hundred thousand pounds, and the shareholders were owed two hundred thousand pounds. The brewer Samuel Whitbread took control of the finances and the plans for rebuilding, but he excluded Sheridan from them.

After the assassination of the Prime Minister in 1812 Parliament was dissolved. Sheridan decided he could not stand for Ilchester again, as, if he did, he could not support Catholic Emancipation in Ireland. He stood instead for Stafford, but failed to be re-elected. There followed an unhappy incident when money given by the Prince Regent to purchase Sheridan another seat seemed to have been diverted to pay his debts. It is hard to discover what actually did happen, but it was a sad business since it effectively ended Sheridan's friendship with the Prince Regent.

Now he was no longer an MP, Sheridan could be arrested for debt — and was, in 1814. Whitbread got him released from the spunging-house, but his last years were often miserable. He worried about his son Tom's health, and his drunkenness alienated many of his friends. By 1816 his own health was bad. He was 'undone and broken-hearted', he wrote to his friend the poet Samuel Rogers (1763–1855); he was afraid that the bailiffs would seize him. His London house at 17 Savile Road was stripped of furniture and he and his wife (who was dying of cancer) were in bed, ill. It was a miserable situation, alleviated by some of his friends only at the last minute. He died, at the age of sixty-five, on 7 July 1816.

The ironical aspect of his last days was that when he died he had reduced his vast debts to a little over five thousand pounds. He had settled money on his wife which amounted to forty thousand pounds.

Friends, who had not realised his needs—or had not helped him if they did—flocked to his funeral. 'Without means, without connexion', Lord Byron (1788–1824) wrote to Thomas Moore, 'he beat them all, in all he ever attempted'. Sheridan had been a mixture: both indolent and energetic, both hospitable and easy going, both kind and vain; he chose Parliament for his arena, preferring to be a politician than a writer or a player upon the stage. There had been times when he reached the level of statesmanship, but the irony of it was that his real achievement was in the world of the theatre which he disliked. His place in Westminster Abbey beside the author and actor David Garrick was the most fitting one.

The stage in Sheridan's day

In the second half of the eighteenth century the stage was still affected by the change of taste that had been marked by the Reverend Jeremy Collier's *A Short View of the Immorality and Profaneness of the English Stage* (1698). This was an attack upon the comic drama which flourished after the Restoration of Charles II in 1660. Restoration comedy had been motivated by reaction against the puritanism which had closed the theatres in 1642; its comedies of manners were often not only witty, but heartless and immoral. There was some justice in the clergyman's pamphlet, as John Dryden (1631–1700), one of the successful dramatists, admitted. Both William Congreve (1670–1729) and Sir John Vanbrugh defended their kind of comedy in print, but not very effectively. Indeed the time for it was over, for the audience had changed from being aristocratic; the theatre was no longer a meeting-place for courtiers (and, often, courtesans). At the Restoration courtiers—the Duke of Buckingham, Sir Robert Howard, Sir Charles Sedley, the Earl of Orrery and the Earl of Rochester, for example—had written plays; they were interested in French drama, which had so influenced the Restoration stage in England. The Restoration had given women greater freedom in society, and on the stage women's parts were now played by women, not boys, as in Elizabethan and Jacobean days.

The comedies of the Restoration had been more concerned with manners than with morals. But by the turn of the century the audience was a middle-class one, imbued with bourgeois respectability, and it wanted a very different kind of drama. Wit and artistry mattered less than sensibility, sentimentality and melodrama. Ruthlessness was replaced by a greater degree of humanity, as can be seen in the comedies of George Farquhar (1677–1707), who, in *The Recruiting Officer* (1706) and *The Beaux' Stratagem* (1707) moved the action out of London—'the Town'—to country towns and houses. Fashion was no longer all; instead of witty, fashionable attitudes there was more evidence of kindness, more understanding of the plight of lovers, more amicability between parents and children.

In 1737 the theatre came under the control of a Licensing Act, introduced by the Prime Minister, Walpole, largely because his Government had been effectively satirised by Henry Fielding (1707–54) in various burlesques. This Act laid down that the Lord Chamberlain should have plays submitted for his approval fourteen days before they were acted. Two theatres only, Drury Lane and Covent Garden, were allowed to present spoken drama (which became known as 'the legitimate' as a result). These two patent theatres had thenceforth to compete with the lighter offerings of the minor theatres: spectacles, burlettas, and other forms of variety. And a dramatist had, as a result, to please a new kind of audience. The day of the private patron was over; the public was the dramatists' new patron. It was less well educated, and it demanded to be entertained. But it was an audience with puritanical attitudes which would not tolerate overt indecency.

There were changes in the organisation of the theatre. The old methods of actors holding shares in a company was replaced by the new one, of managers who engaged actors and paid them salaries. The managers chose the plays to be performed, and thus exercised control over the dramatists, whose fortunes also depended upon the performance of the actors and actresses. In the early part of the century the style of acting had become somewhat unexpressive, stereotyped and mannered; it took David Garrick (1717–79) to humanise it, to make it effective. The theatres themselves were changing. The lighting had been improved (bills for candles, for instance, were very large, and economies in selling candle-ends efficiently were very real) with greater risks of fire; there was a tendency towards the picture-frame stage, though Drury Lane's fore-stage (or apron stage) still projected about fourteen feet into the auditorium, thus making the use of asides still viable. The proscenium doors were placed next to the stage boxes. The use of sliding scenery (probably set in grooves) was developed, and allowed more spectacular productions.

As a result of all these changes in the nature of the audience and the theatre, dramatists wrote comedies which suited both the public's taste and the standards of the Lord Chamberlain: the plays tended to be refined, sentimental and even at times didactic, their authors striving to improve taste and standards of behaviour. As a result little of the comedy produced has survived; it lacked the ruthless wit, the sparkle and ebullient energy, and the contrast between appearance and reality which had informed many earlier Restoration comedies. There are, however, notable exceptions: in particular Farquhar's plays, from the early years of the century, survive and still please modern audiences because they are funny, fast-moving and unexpected; and so do the comedies of

Goldsmith and Sheridan. All three writers were Irish. Both Oliver Goldsmith (1728–74) and Sheridan loathed sentimental comedy and indeed denounced it effectively upon occasion, Goldsmith writing an essay on it, Sheridan mocking it in the new prologue he wrote for the second production of *The Rivals* and parodying it in *The Critic*.

Goldsmith began with *The Good-Natur'd Man* (1768), which was amusing, full of satire and self-exposure on the part of the hero, whose good nature nearly ruins him. The plot was complicated, and the audience disliked the scenes with bailiffs which were thought 'low'. His next comedy, however, *She Stoops to Conquer* (1773), was outstandingly successful and is still frequently performed. In it Goldsmith utilised an experience of his own when he was a schoolboy; he thought a house belonging to a friend of his father was an inn, and behaved arrogantly in it. This is the basis of the plot in his play where one of the heroes is a man shy in the company of ladies of quality but at his ease with barmaids. He thinks that he is in an inn and behaves accordingly. He is, however, in the house of his father's friend, whose daughter he is intended to marry. There is another pair of lovers , and the inhabitants of the house, all unusual characters, include Tony Lumpkin, a highly effective creation. The plot dashes along, filled with farce, comic wit irradiating the absurdities and anti-climaxes. Goldsmith delighted in contrasts between appearance and reality, and 'the mistakes of a night' are worked out with dashing exuberance.

Sheridan, too, saw the contrast between appearance and reality as a basic ingredient of comedy. But where Goldsmith reminds us of the Elizabethans in his emphasis upon fun and farce, Sheridan's links are with Restoration comedy, suitably toned down for his audience. His sense of social situation, his satiric and witty way of treating his characters, of exposing folly and hypocrisy, his ability to create dramatic crises, his creation of sparkling dialogue, all combine in *The Rivals*, *The School for Scandal* and *The Critic* in a timeless way. They are as fresh now as when they took their London audiences by storm in the late eighteenth century. And, curiously enough, the same comic invention, the same satiric sense was to blossom in the nineteenth century in the work of two other Irish dramatists, Oscar Wilde (1854–1900) and George Bernard Shaw (1856–1950), who brought life and the explosive energy of wit back on to the London stage in the way Goldsmith and Sheridan had virtually a century before.

A note on the text

The Rivals was first printed in 1775 after the second performance of the play, on 28 January, had ensured its success. There were two octavo editions in 1775, the first carelessly printed, and the second a reprint of it.

A Dublin duodecimo edition appeared in 1775. The 'third edition corrected' was issued in 1776. Thomas Moore used this third edition for his text of *The Works of the late Richard Brinsley Sheridan*, 2 volumes, 1821. The text of the play, as it was originally submitted for the Lord Chamberlain's licence on 9 January 1775 (and first produced on 17 January 1775) exists in the Larpent MS, now in the Huntington Library, San Marino, California; it was edited by R.L. Purdy, Clarendon Press, Oxford, 1935.

There is a good edition of *The Rivals* in *The Plays and Poems of Richard Brinsley Sheridan*, ed. R. Crompton Rhodes, Clarendon Press, Oxford, 3 vols, 1928; reprinted New York, 1962, and another in *British Dramatists from Dryden to Sheridan*, ed. George H. Nettleton and Authur E. Case, Harrap, London, 1939. Both of these, however, are superseded by the excellent edition of the play in *The Dramatic Works of Richard Brinsley Sheridan*, ed. C.J.L. Price, Oxford University Press, Oxford, 2 vols, 1973. Two easily available modern editions are *The Rivals*, ed. A. Norman Jeffares (English Classics—New Series), Macmillan, London, 1967; St Martins Press, New York, 1967 (this contains an appendix with passages from the Larpent MS to show the kind of material Sheridan altered or excised after the first performance, refining the characters of Sir Lucius O'Trigger and Sir Anthony Absolute, tightening up the action and actually adding new material); and *The Rivals*, edited C.J.L. Price, Oxford University Press, London, 1968 (this contains the prologue for the first night, taken from the Amelia Edwards Collection, Somerville College, Oxford).

Part 2

Summaries
of THE RIVALS

A general summary

The play is set in Bath, where the action takes place in one day. Bath is a fashionable resort, frequented by 'people of distinction', whose servants reveal the basic secret of the plot to us in the first scene. Lydia Languish, a wealthy girl, is in love with Captain Jack Absolute, son and heir of Sir Anthony Absolute. Sir Anthony, we are told, is gouty, and will be surprised to know his son is in Bath. But in order to play up to Lydia's romantic notions, Captain Jack Absolute is pretending to be an ensign on half-pay, calling himself Beverley. We are also told that there is 'a tough old aunt in the way'. Fag, Captain Absolute's (or the supposed Ensign Beverley's) servant, is reminded by the coachman that Faulkland (who is in Bath at present) is to marry Lydia's cousin Julia Melville, (who has just come to Bath with Sir Anthony). Lucy, Lydia's maid, to whom Captain Absolute is giving a bribe, is also introduced. Fag indicates to the coachman how fashionable even the servants are at Bath.

The second scene satirises the vogue for reading sentimental novels in a conversation between Lydia and Lucy, her maid. Lydia tells Julia that her aunt, Mrs Malaprop, has intercepted a note from her written to Ensign Beverley, and that she has confined Lydia to the house ever since. But Mrs Malaprop, she says, has herself fallen in love with an Irish baronet, Sir Lucius O'Trigger, and corresponds with him under the feigned name of Delia. And Bob Acres, a neighbour of the Absolutes, is also in Bath. But to add to all her news, Lydia tells Julia that she had quarrelled with Beverley before her aunt found out about their secret correspondence, and she fears she has lost Beverley for ever. She also tells Julia that she loses most of her fortune of thirty thousand pounds if she marries without her aunt's consent before she comes of age, that she has determined to do this, and that she could never love any man who would wish 'to wait a day for the alternative'. Julia thinks her capricious, but is teased by Lydia about the nature of her jealous fiancé Faulkland, who had saved her from drowning, and does not yet know she has arrived in Bath.

Julia leaves when Lucy says that Sir Anthony Absolute and Mrs Malaprop are arriving. Lydia and Lucy hide the novels. Mrs Malaprop attacks Lydia for her liking for Ensign Beverley and sends her to her room. After agreeing on the evils of circulating libraries Sir Anthony discusses with Mrs Malaprop the possibility of his son Jack Absolute as a suitor for Lydia. Mrs Malaprop agrees, says she will get rid of Mr Acres (who has been described as 'odious' by Lydia earlier). After Sir Anthony leaves, Mrs Malaprop reveals that she is motivated by annoyance that Lydia knows of her feelings for Sir Lucius O'Trigger. She summons Lucy, whom she trusts, telling her she will give her a letter for Sir Lucius. And Lucy reveals to the audience how she has been bribed by Lydia, by Beverley, by Mrs Malaprop (to whom she betrayed Lydia and Beverley), by Bob Acres (for carrying letters she never delivered) and by Sir Lucius O'Trigger (who believes he is corresponding with the niece, not the aunt).

The second act introduces Captain Absolute; Fag tells him of his father's arrival in Bath and how his presence has been explained to Sir Anthony by Fag as due to recruiting duties. Then Faulkland enters and we learn something of his character as well as of Jack Absolute's fear that Lydia would not accept him if she were to find he is a Captain with the reversion of a good fortune, that she would prefer to elope with him as Ensign Beverley rather than marry him in an ordinary way. We learn of Faulkland's sentimental worries about Julia: his jealousy is stirred by the arrival of Bob Acres, who tells him she is in good health, 'the bell and spirit of the Company wherever she has been'. He leaves and we learn more of Acres, who tells Jack how he is infuriated by Ensign Beverley's (whom he does not know) pursuing Lydia. He too leaves, and Sir Anthony arrives to inform Jack that he has found a suitable person for him to marry. When Jack demurs and says his affections are otherwise engaged Sir Anthony bursts into a fury and says that he will disinherit him if he does not agree to do as his father requires within six and a half hours. After he leaves Jack passes on his irritation to Fag, who in turn bullies the errand-boy.

The second scene reveals Lucy busy at her intrigues; she gives Sir Lucius O'Trigger a letter from Mrs Malaprop; then she asks Fag to tell his master (Ensign Beverley) that Sir Anthony has proposed his son as a suitor for Lydia—she described him as a worse rival than Acres.

The third act opens with Jack Absolute relishing the extraordinary situation that his father wants to force him to marry the girl with whom he is planning to run away. There follows an absurd interchange where Jack agrees to marry his father's choice. In the second scene Julia, exasperated by Faulkland's jealous doubts of her affection, leaves in tears, whereupon Faulkland realises how silly he has been. The third scene opens with Mrs Malaprop showing Jack Absolute a letter which Ensign Beverley had written to Lydia. In this he had abused Mrs Malaprop, and suggested that he had a scheme of making Mrs Malaprop, 'the old harridan', a go-between. Ironically she does, in fact, bring about a meeting between the two lovers. When Lydia comes in and greets him as Beverley, Absolute tells her that he has pretended to be Captain Absolute, and makes a romantic speech persuading her to run away with him. Mrs Malaprop overhears them, and bursts in when Lydia is saying that her aunt's choice can be Captain Absolute but hers is Beverley. Lydia denies she had said to Absolute's face that she loved another better (since she thinks he is Beverley). At this Mrs Malaprop, in a great rage, takes her away.

The fourth scene reveals Acres, trying to make himself fit for the social life of Bath. When his friend Sir Lucius arrives Acres tells him he has a rival for Lydia's affections in Ensign Beverley whom he does not know. Sir Lucius suggests that Acres should challenge him to a duel, but says that he himself cannot take the challenge to Ensign Beverley for Acres as he has another similar affair on his hands with a captain who has 'put a jest' on him lately.

The first scene of the fourth act begins with a conversation between Acres and his servant, who are discussing the dangers of duelling. Acres is worried, but can't allow his servant to persuade him not to fight. Absolute comes in and Acres asks him to convey a challenge to Beverley; he agrees, but says it would not be proper for him to act as second to Acres. He leaves promising to tell Beverley that Acres is a 'determined dog', that he is called 'Fighting Bob'.

Scene 2 complicates matters. Mrs Malaprop and Lydia are at cross purposes—Mrs Malaprop praising Absolute, Lydia praising Beverley—when Sir Anthony and Captain Absolute are announced. Lydia says she won't speak to or look at the Captain. Neither of the young people responds to being urged to address the other. Finally Captain Absolute speaks in a low, hoarse voice, hoping Lydia will not recognise him as Beverley, but in vain; finally all is out, and Sir Anthony and Mrs Malaprop decide to forget and forgive them the deception. But once the lovers are left alone Lydia and Jack quarrel, she accusing him of deception, of treating her like a child. When Sir Anthony and Mrs Malaprop return, she renounces him for ever. Sir Anthony thinks his son has been over-eager in his advances, despite Jack's denials, and the scene ends with Sir Anthony saying Mrs Malaprop must make his peace with Lydia for him.

The third scene opens with Sir Lucius searching for Captain Absolute. He enters, furious with Lydia's treatment of him, is met by Sir Lucius who forces a quarrel on him, and agrees to meet him at King's Mead Fields at about six o'clock to settle the matter. Sir Lucius departs and Faulkland then arrives, to be asked to second Absolute. He hears of Absolute's disappointment with Lydia, and tells him of his own bad treatment of Julia. Just then a servant brings him a forgiving letter from Julia, but he immediately shifts into suspicion of her again.

In the beginning of the fifth act Faulkland visits Julia to say farewell, telling her he has to avoid a quarrel by leaving the country; actually he is testing her reactions. When she receives his news with utter loyalty and devotion, a readiness to devote her resources to supporting them both in exile (irrespective of whether or not his fortune is forfeited by his act), he tells her that he has invented the whole thing but is now completely convinced and content. This is too much for her to accept. She tells him that Absolute and Beverley are the same person. Their conversation is also. Lydia comes to Julia for consolation. Julia does not tell her of her own troubles, but does say that she had been informed by Faulkland that Absolute and Beverley are the same person. There conversation is interrupted by the arrival of Mrs Malaprop, Fag and David, Acres' servant, with the news that Absolute, Acres, Faulkland and Sir Lucius are involved in duelling. They all rush off to try to prevent mischief, David being sent to find Sir Anthony.

In the second scene Sir Anthony meets his son, who tries to avoid him by pretending to be someone else. Captain Absolute is hiding a sword which, when Sir Anthony discovers it, he pretends to be bringing to Lydia, with the idea of swearing to her that he will fall on its point if she won't forgive him. Sir Anthony thinks the gesture may work, and sends him on his way. But then David runs in and tells Sir Anthony of the fighting planned in King's Mead Fields. Sir Anthony and he leave together, hoping to stop the duelling.

The third scene is set in King's Mead Fields, with Sir Lucius advising Acres on how he is to fight, while Acres is becoming more anxious every moment. When Faulkland and Absolute arrive the matter of Beverley's identity is clarified, and Acres horrifies Sir Lucius by saying he does not want to fight his dear friend Jack Absolute. Then, as Sir Lucius and Absolute draw their swords to settle their affair, Sir Anthony, David and the women arrive. When Lydia offers her hand to Jack, Sir Lucius accepts his apology for an affront of which Absolute was unaware and which he had never intended, but then begins to challenge Lydia about the letters he thinks she has written him as Delia. Mrs Malaprop admits she wrote the letters and Sir Lucius receives the news politely, but says to Captain Absolute that, to show he is not ungrateful, since he has taken that lady from him he will give him his Delia into the bargain. Next Julia forgives Faulkland, and Acres asks them all to a party; the lovers make speeches on how their troubles have turned into unalloyed happiness.

Detailed summaries

Preface to the first edition

Sheridan argues that a play's reputation is made by its performance on the stage, so that a preface by the author is unnecessary. If a play has not been well received in the theatre, then a preface by its author pleading its cause illustrates the weakness of that cause. He would not have written a preface himself were it not for the fact that the success of his play was unusual.

What was unusual was that the play was withdrawn and revised and then succeeded. Sheridan points out his own inexperience and lack of judgement when he wrote *The Rivals*. He defends the management of the theatre from the charge that they should not have put on a play which was unusually long. He says that he was told it was too long, but he thought that Mr Harris, the manager, was over-kind to him because he had already altered so much in the play that he did not want to upset a young author's self-respect by insisting on further pruning. He adds as a further explanation of the first night's failure that his desire to be original led him astray.

He was surprised, he says, not so much by the audience's unfavourable reaction to particular parts of the play as by his own failure to see that these passages deserved such a reaction. It was suggested to him that some of the unfavourable criticism arose out of malice.

He argues that an author should, to a certain extent, defer to an audience's opinion; but puny little critics, on the other hand, are not worthy of notice. He defends himself from the accusation that he had reflected on the Irish character in his creation of Sir Lucius O'Trigger, and ends by thanking the actors and praising the managers of the theatre.

NOTES AND GLOSSARY:

closet-prologue: a prologue intended for reading in a study or private room

tribunal: a court or place of judgement

the withdrawing of the piece: *The Rivals* was first performed on 17 January 1775; it was withdrawn and heavily revised before its second performance eleven days later

extreme inexperience: Sheridan was only twenty-three when *The Rivals*, his first play, was produced

Mr Harris: the manager of Covent Garden Theatre, where *The Rivals* was first performed

the attack on the piece: the *London Chronicle*, 21–24 January, 1775, reported that several people who were evidently planted in the galleries 'to disturb the performance, were turned out before the last act'. The *Morning Chronicle* and *London Advertiser* of 20 January had described the fuss as 'a little malice from one corner of the gallery' which showed itself 'too early to produce any effect'

subjects on which the mind has been much informed: the *Monthly Review*, February 1775, in the course of a favourable review of *The Rivals*, objected to Sheridan's dreading imitation, arguing that invention cannot exist until the mind is stored with information

national reflection ... Sir Lucius O'Trigger: Sheridan was attacked in a letter in the *Morning Post* on 21 January 1775 for 'an ungenerous attack upon a nation' in this 'villainous portrait of an Irish gentleman'

stage-novels: probably the type of sentimental comedy which Sheridan disliked so much and satirised in the behaviour and speeches of Julia and Faulkland

---

Prologue

The first prologue is a conversation between two lawyers. The Attorney persuades the Serjeant at Law to plead the poet's (Sheridan's) case before the court (the audience in the theatre).

NOTES AND GLOSSARY:
These notes and glossaries relate to the prologue given in the third edition (see 'A note on the text' p.13); the text of the prologue for the first night is printed only in C.J. Price's edition of 1968.

Serjeant at Law: a barrister

Attorney: a solicitor

giving a paper: barristers receive legal work from solicitors

cramp hand: cramped handwriting

a poet's brief: the play. A brief is the summary of facts in a legal case prepared for the instruction of a barrister by a solicitor

plead the Muse's cause: you would represent the Muse. In the prologue cited in C.J.L. Price's edition of 1968 the lines 'A student erring from the Temple grounds/Pleads to a trespass on the Muse's grounds' mean that Sheridan who had studied law was taking to writing drama

sons of Phoebus: poets. The Greek god Phoebus Apollo was the god of poetry

the Fleet: a debtors' prison in London (demolished in 1845)

bays: poet's garlands were traditionally made of bay leaves and laurel

his legal waste of wig: the wig he wore as a barrister

full-bottomed: the shoulder-length wig worn by judges and by King's (or Queen's) Counsel on state occasions

your client: the poet

This wig ... warmer ... bays: it pays better to be a lawyer than a poet

flourish: to use florid language

Serjeant Woodward: the actor Ned Woodward, who played Captain Absolute in the first production. The prologue printed in Price's edition reads 'Serjeant Lewis', that is, W.T. Lewis (1748?–1811) who acted the part of Faulkland

dread *court*: the audience in the theatre

equity: that which is fair and right (also a system of law existing side by side with common or statue law, superseding them when they come into conflict with it)

flaw: although guilty, to escape by some legal technicality

writ of error: permission to have a case tried again in another court because of some unfairness in the circumstances of the first trial

Drury Lane: there were only two patent theatres in London at the time, Drury Lane and Covent Garden, in which plays could be performed legally (but their monopoly was often infringed)

costs of suit: if the winner of a legal action is awarded judgement with costs he can recover from his opponent all or part of the cost of bringing the action

spleen: bad temper

transportation: up to 1868 criminals who escaped the gallows (being executed by hanging) were sentenced to be transported to the colonies

a groan—*damnation!*: a failure of a play on its first night. This nearly happened to *The Rivals* on its first night

right of challenge: before a legal action begins, a party in a case has the right to challenge any member of the jury and have him removed if sufficient cause is shown

newsman: a writer of a newsletter, a journalist

Second prologue

The second prologue refers to the earlier one. The single speaker says that since the poet's case (in which the serjeant at law of the earlier prologue took part) has been won—in other words since the play has been a great success (this prologue was written for the tenth night of the play's performance, an unusually long run for the time)—she will serve the Muse instead. She points to the figure of Comedy, and asks whether she should preach, arguing that the Muse of Comedy should not be grave, and how should the sentimental Muse be allowed to displace her, because if she were to do so she would end her weeping comedies in violence.

The critic and the poet are both needed to keep comedy free of sentimentality, but tragedy can, when attacked, in turn attack the idea of guilt.

NOTES AND GLOSSARY:

tenth night:	at the time a run of ten performances of a play was very successful
granted our cause:	because the play had run for ten performances the author's case was won
Serjeant:	a reference to the speaker of the first prologue
the Muse:	of comedy
this form:	the figure of Comedy, to which the speaker (Mrs Bulkley, who played Julia in the first performance) points
light mask:	the mask of comedy (a reference to the wearing of different kinds of masks in ancient Greek comedy and tragedy)
the sentimental Muse:	Sheridan, like his compatriot Oliver Goldsmith (1728–74), attacked sentimental comedy
the Pilgrim's Progress:	a reference to *The Pilgrim's Progress* (1678, and 2nd and 3rd edn., 1679) by John Bunyan (1628–88), a moral allegory
rue:	an evergreen shrub, an emblem of repentance or grief
fixed in usurpation:	lifeless sentimental comedy has usurped tragedy and comedy
the dagger:	an emblem of Melpomene, the Muse of Tragedy
vot'ries:	votaries, people bound by a vow, devoted followers
Harry Woodward:	the actor who played the Serjeant
Dunstal, Quick, Ned Shuter, Barsanti, Mrs Green:	actors and actresses in the play
their fav'rite:	the favourite of Virtue and Truth is the figure of Tragedy; the speaker is pointing to the figure of Tragedy
poniard:	small dagger

Dramatis personae

NOTES AND GLOSSARY:

Scene—Bath:	a fashionable resort in the south west of England, famous for its waters

Time of Action: the first edition reads 'Time of Action, Five Hours', the third edition 'Time of Action, within One Day'. Sheridan is obeying one of the unities, the three principles of dramatic composition: that a play should consist of one main action occurring at one time (not longer than the play takes in performance) and in one place. Aristotle (384–322BC) put this idea in his *Poetics* and sixteenth-century Italian critics and seventeenth-century French classical dramatists developed and adapted it

---

Act 1 Scene 1

This scene, set in a street in Bath, introduces the situations of the main characters through a conversation between Fag, Captain Jack Absolute's servant, and a fellow servant, Thomas, the coachman, who is a servant of Jack's father, Sir Anthony Absolute. Fag tells the coachman about Jack's pretending to be Ensign Beverley, because he is in love with Lydia Languish, a wealthy girl, who likes him more as a supposed ensign on half-pay than if she were to know he is Sir Anthony's son and heir. Fag also tells the coachman that there is a troublesome aunt who does not know Jack Absolute. We next hear about fashionable Bath from the servants' point of view; we are told of Faulkland's being engaged to Julia Melville, and that the Captain is giving money to Lucy, Lydia's maid. Sheridan conveys vital information about the characters and the plot very efficiently in this scene.

NOTES AND GLOSSARY:

Od's life!:	probably a corruption of 'God's life'
postillion:	the rider of the near leading horse of a carriage or post-chaise drawn by four horses
gi't:	give it
whip!:	suddenly! quick!, an exclamation, suited to the coachman, implying speedy action (as when a whip was applied to horses)
Ensign:	the lowest rank of commissioned officer, a sub-lieutenant, in the infantry; he carried the ensign or standard
LOVE:	he spells out the word
Jupiter:	in classical mythology the chief of the Gods (also known as Zeus); he pursued human maidens, using various disguises: as a shower of gold (with Danaë); as a satyr (with Antiope); as a swan (with Leda); and as a bull (with Europa)

Hark'ee: hearken, listen

singular: peculiar, odd

half-pay ensign: the army was maintained at half-pay during periods of peace

stocks: money lent to the government. The British government consolidated various loan stocks into a single stock in 1751, at a uniform rate of interest: hence 'Consols'

Zounds!: a corruption of 'God's wounds'

the national debt: money borrowed by the government in exchange for stock

thread papers: papers round which thread or silk was wound

a set of thousands: the coachman may be suggesting that Captain Absolute is only one (of a set of) thousands who are pursuing her. It has also been suggested that it could mean a set of horses worth thousands of pounds, but it probably means that the thread papers, made of banknotes, are worth thousands of pounds

draw kindly with: pull together with, agree with. The coachman is using a phrase from his own trade, relating to a horse and mare pulling together when drawing a coach

pigeons: turtle doves, noted for affection for their mates

Gloucestershire: an English county

mort: (*dialect*) a great deal, great amount

'tis a good lounge: a place to relax

pump room: a place at a spa where the medical waters are dispensed

the waters: the famous hot springs of Bath

card after eleven: Beau Nash (1674–1761) when Master of Ceremonies at Bath decreed that the day's entertainments should end at eleven p.m.

gentleman: valet, personal servant

Du-Peigne: *peigne* is French for comb, and French valets were then fashionable

any degree of *ton*: any amount of *ton* (*French*), manner in general, style, fashion

took to their own hair: gave up wearing wigs

Od rabbit it: an imprecation, probably from 'God rat (rot) it'

the Bar ... the Box: refers to lawyers; but it can also mean the bar of the carriage used in mounting to the box. The box is the coachman's seat. The meaning is that fashion affecting lawyers spreads to coachmen

tho'ff: though (probably a vulgar pronunciation)

Jack Gauge the Exciseman: an exciseman, or revenue officer, gauged (measured) the contents of casks

ta'en to his carrots: wearing his own red hair

Dick the farrier: a farrier shoes (and cures ailments in) horses

bob: a bob-peruke, a wig kept close to the head with its bottom locks turned up in short curls

the college: the College of Physicians or the College of Surgeons, professional institutions to which Doctors belong

Zooks!: an exclamation, a contraction for 'Gadzooks', perhaps for 'God's hooks' or nails

Gyde's porch: these old assembly Rooms on the Lower Walks in Bath were kept by a Mr Gyde

---

Act 1 Scene 2

The second scene begins with Lucy delivering novels she has got for her mistress, Lydia Languish, at the circulating libraries. Julia Melville arrives, to be told that Lydia's connection with Beverley has been discovered, her aunt Mrs Malaprop having intercepted a note. Lydia further tells Julia that Mrs Malaprop is corresponding, under the name of Delia, with Sir Lucius O'Trigger, an Irish baronet with whom she has fallen in love, but who does not know that she is Delia. Lydia is also disturbed by the arrival of Bob Acres in Bath, and, worst of all, she quarrelled with Beverley the day before her aunt found out about their friendship and confined her to the house. We learn that Lydia has to have her aunt's consent if she marries before she is of age; otherwise she will lose most of her fortune—she has, however, decided she wishes to marry without her aunt's consent, an idea Julia regards as caprice.

Julia has her own problems; she was engaged to marry Faulkland before her father's death; but he does not think he is sufficiently loved by her. Lydia teases her about this. Julia leaves when she hears Sir Anthony Absolute has arrived, and she prepares the audience for Mrs Malaprop's oddity by referring to her misapplication of words. Lydia tells Lucy to hide the novels and replace them with various moral works. Mrs Malaprop tries—in vain—to make Lydia promise to give up Beverley and then sends her to her room. Sir Anthony denounces circulating libraries. Then he and Mrs Malaprop discuss Lydia's future. Mrs Malaprop says there there is no commitment to Bob Acres as a suitor, that, as Lydia is so set against him, Sir Anthony's son may have better success. He leaves, saying Jack dare not object to his father's plans.

Mrs Malaprop tells Lucy to come shortly to collect a letter for Sir Lucius and leaves. Then Lucy reveals her duplicity; she has had money and clothes from Lydia for helping in her plan to run off with Ensign

Beverley; she has had money from Beverley; she has had money and a garment from Mrs Malaprop for betraying Lydia and Beverley to her; she has had money and a pair of buckles from Mr Acres for carrying letters (which she never delivered); she has had money and a snuff box from Sir Lucius O'Trigger, and has tricked him into believing he was corresponding not with the aunt but with the niece.

NOTES AND GLOSSARY:

Mrs Malaprop's lodging: the name comes from French *mal à propos*, inappropriate, unsuitable

circulating library: books kept by a bookseller and lent out for a fee

The Reward of Constancy: possibly *The Happy Pair, or, Virtue and Constancy Rewarded* (1771)

The Fatal Connection: a novel by Mrs Fogerty (2 vols, 1773)

The Mistakes of the Heart: a novel by Pierre Henri Treyssac de Vergy, *The Mistakes of the Heart, or, Memoirs of Lady Caroline Pelham and Lady Victoria Nevil* (3 vols, 1769)

Mr Bull   Lewis Bull, a bookseller in Bath, who owned a circulating library opposite Gyde's Porch

The Delicate Distress: The Delicate Distress and The Gordian Knot By the Authors of Henry and Frances (1769–70); the first was a novel by Mrs Elizabeth Griffith (1793), the second by her husband Richard Griffith (1788)

The Memoirs of Lady Woodford: written by herself (1771)

Mr Frederick: a bookseller who worked in Bath from 1745 to 1772; he gave up his circulating library in 1770

dog's eared it: turned down the corners of its pages (to mark where the reader had stopped reading or wanted to remember a page)

child: Lydia is being pleasant to her maid

The Gordian Knot: see note on *The Delicate Distress* above

Peregrine Pickle: *The Adventures of Peregrine Pickle* (1751) by Tobias Smollett (1721–71)

The Tears of Sensibility: four French novels by Baculard D'Arnaud (1716–1805), translated by John Murdoch (2 vols, 1773)

Humphrey Clinker: The Expedition of Humphrey Clinker (1771) by Tobias Smollett

The Memoirs of a Lady of Quality, written by herself: supposed to be by Lady Vane; included in Smollett's *Peregrine Pickle*

The Sentimental Journey: A Sentimental Journey through France and Italy (2 vols, 1768) by Laurence Sterne (1713–68), the author of *Tristram Shandy* (1759–67)

The Whole Duty of Man: a very popular work of piety by Richard Allestree (1618–91) published in 1659. In the next two hundred years more than forty editions of it were issued. C.J. Price comments in his edition that Lucy may be referring to the large folio editions of 1704 or 1723 since she describes it as the 'great one'

press a few blonds: blonds, blonde lace made from unbleached silk formed in hexagonal mesh. The implication is that the book is not read

sal volatile: an aromatic solution of ammonium carbonate used to restore people who had fainted. It was either drunk, as sal volatile, or sniffed, in the form of smelling salts

conjured: brought you here magically

dressed: formally dressed (that is, not in his travelling clothes)

rout: a large party, social gathering

Delia or Celia: these names were often used by poets in the seventeenth and eighteenth centuries to conceal the identities of their mistresses

Apropos: on the present subject

fopperies: refinements

unhackneyed: not over-used to

a water spaniel: a gun-dog with long frilled ears, silky coat, used for starting and retrieving game

misapplied ... mispronounced: Sheridan may have based his character of Mrs Malaprop upon Mrs Tryfort in a comedy by his mother, *A Journey to Bath.* Mrs Tryfort was described as the 'vainest poor creature', who was fond of 'hard words which, without miscalling, she always takes care to misapply'

O lud!: O Lord!

coz: cousin, a term of affection

toilet: dressing-table

Roderick Random: *The Adventures of Roderick Random* (1748), another novel by Tobias Smollett

The Innocent Adultery: probably a translation (1722) made by Samuel Croxall of *L'Adultère Innocente* by the French novelist Paul Scarron (1610–60), who was the husband of Madame de Maintenon (R.C. Rhodes in his edition of Sheridan's *Plays and Poems*, 1928, argued it was *Harriet, or The Innocent Adultress,* 1771)

Lord Aimsworth: possibly *The History of Lord Aimsworth, and the Honourable Charles Hartford, Esq., in a Series of Letters* by the author of *Dorinda Catsby*, and *Ermina, or the Fair Recluse* (2 vols, 1773)

Ovid: Publius Ovidius Naso (43BC–AD17). The Roman poet Ovid was frequently translated, and Lydia was probably reading the *Amores*, or the *Metamorphoses* or the *Heroides*, mainly letters supposedly written by noble ladies to absent husbands or lovers

The Man of Feeling: a sentimental novel (1771) by the Scottish novelist and dramatist Henry Mackenzie (1745–1831)

Mrs Chapone: *Letters on the Improvement of the Mind, Addressed to a Young Lady* (1773), a book of essays by Hester Chapone (1727–1801)

Fordyce's Sermons: *Sermons to Young Women* (1765) by James Fordyce (1720–96)

hairdresser has torn away: the book's pages have been used for curling papers

Lord Chesterfield's Letters: *Letters written by the late Right Honourable Philip Dormer Stanhope, Earl of Chesterfield, to his son, Philip Stanhope, Esq* (2 vols, 1774)

illiterate: obliterate. Mrs Malaprop sometimes uses a word resembling the word she intends, sometimes uses high sounding words which are only haphazardly appropriate. It is not always possible to suggest what word she intends

extirpate: extricate (or, possibly, exculpate)

controvertible: incontrovertible

blackamoor: Negro

intricate: ingrate (or, possibly, obstinate)

the black art: witchcraft, magic

misanthropy: misanthropist

half bound ... marble covers!: books with the back or spine and the corners of the cover bound in leather, with the rest in paper boards resembling marble

evergreen tree of knowledge: a reference to the tree 'of the knowledge of good and evil' in the Bible, Genesis 2:17

laconically: ironically

progeny: prodigy

Simony: a term for buying and selling ecclesiastical livings. Does Mrs Malaprop mean 'ciphering'?

Fluxions: she probably means fractions. Fluxions is a term used in Newtonion calculus

Paradoxes:	possibly parallax
diabolical:	she probably puts in this word for the sound of it
supercilious:	superficial
geometry:	geography
contagious:	contiguous
orthodoxy:	orthography
reprehend:	apprehend
superstitious:	superfluous
conciliating:	possibly constricting
illegible:	ineligible
keep a tight hand:	a metaphor from riding or driving, to keep a tight hand on the reins, to control effectively
intuition:	tuition
artificial:	artful
you was:	fashionable usage for 'you were'
O Gemini!:	the twins Castor and Pollux, a sign of the Zodiac or the constellation named after them, though the phrase could be a corruption of *Jesu domine*
malevolence:	benevolence
locality:	loquacity
paduasoy:	from the French *pou-de-soie*, poudesoy, a strong corded or grosgrain fabric of silk, worn (by both sexes) in the eighteenth century
pocket-pieces:	coins (usually out of circulation, or spurious) carried as lucky charms in the pocket
Hibernian:	an Irishman (from Hibernia, (*Latin*) Ireland)

Act 2 Scene 1

The scene is set in Captain Absolute's lodgings, where Fag reports to his master that Sir Anthony now knows his son is in Bath. Fag has told him a lie, that the Captain is on a recruiting mission in the town—and he lies to his master, too, pretending that he has not told Thomas the coachman the real reason that Captain Absolute is in Bath.

Faulkland enters and Absolute explains to him his plans for gradually letting Lydia know who he really is, because, while he is convinced she would elope with him as Ensign Beverley he is not certain she would marry him in an orthodox way. He does not want to run off with her because that would mean the loss of two-thirds of her fortune.

Faulkland then explains why he is in low spirits; he is worried about Julia, and Absolute gets him to say that if he were to be convinced she were well and in good spirits he would be entirely content. Then Absolute tells him that Julia has just arrived in Bath and is in perfect health. At this point Fag announces that Bob Acres is downstairs.

Absolute explains that Acres is a neighbour of Sir Anthony—and also a rival of himself for Lydia, though Acres does not know that Beverley is Absolute, and indeed has complained to Absolute about Beverley.

Acres enters, is introduced to Faulkland, and tells him that Julia is well and happy. This upsets Faulkland, who thinks she should not be so healthy and happy in his absence. Faulkland becomes more annoyed still when he hears of the kind of songs that Julia has been singing, and learns that she has been dancing country dances, and leaves in a rage. Acres says he is adopting new, smarter ways of dressing, utters threats against Beverley, and describes his new way of swearing.

Acres then leaves and Sir Anthony arrives. He tells his son that he will make him independent and master of a large estate in a few weeks' time. He tells Jack he is to gain this independence and fortune by marrying. Jack asks who the lady is, and when his father, instead of telling him, demands that he promises to love and marry the woman he has chosen for him, informs Sir Anthony that his inclinations are already fixed. There follows an outburst of rage from Sir Anthony, who threatens to disown and disinherit Jack if he does not agree within six and a half hours to do everything his father chooses for him.

After Jack wonders what 'old, wealthy hag' his father wants to bestow on him, Fag comes in to tell him how Sir Anthony has come downstairs and hit him with his cane. Jack pushes Fag out of the way; then Fag, after remarking that it is the vilest injustice when vexed by one person to revenge oneself on another, in his turn attacks an errand-boy.

NOTES AND GLOSSARY:

injectoral:	introduced abruptly, interjectional
'Sdeath:	God's death
to recruit:	the word has several meanings, as Fag goes on to point out
constitution:	health, strength
for men:	for the army
chairmen:	sedan chairs, slung on shafts and made to hold one person, were borne by two chairmen, one at each end
minority waiters:	possibly young, or part-time waiters
billiard markers:	men who kept the score in billiard rooms
whenever I draw on my invention:	Fag resembles a man who draws a bill, that is, requests someone else to pay a sum of money to a third party. That third party can sell the bill (for a smaller sum of money) to some other person, who may require him to endorse it, by signing his name on the back of the bill. He then becomes surety for the bill in the event of the first two not paying

too much security: Fag is inventing the paying agent
indorsements: endorsements, a term coming from mercantile law
reversion: right of inheritance
farrago: medley, confused mixture
aspiration: breath
Odds whips and wheels!: Acres suits his oaths, in 'a new method of swearing', to the subject as he says later in this scene, calling them oaths referential, or sentimental swearing. Here, of course, he relates his oath to his speedy travel
the Mall: a fashionable walk on the north side of St James's Park
I solicit your connections: I wish to become acquainted with you
Od's blushes and blooms!: God's blushes and blooms. Another of Acres's referential oaths, suggesting that Julia is in blooming health
the German Spa: Spa, in the Belgian province of Liège, a resort famous for its restorative, curative, mineral waters
Merry, Od's crickets!: God's crickets! Acres again suits his oath to the images he has of Julia Melville; a cricket is proverbially cheerful
the bell: the belle, the beauty
squallante, rumblante and quiverante: squalling, rumbling and quivering. Acres is inventing words which imitate Italian musical terminology
Od's minnums and crotchets!: God's minims and crotchets! Minims are a half, crotchets a quarter the value of a semibreve in musical notation
Mrs Piano's: as a musical direction *piano* means soft or softly
music the food of love: this echoes the opening line of Shakespeare's *Twelfth Night*: 'If music be the food of love, play on'
purling-stream airs: sentimental songs, like purling, murmuring, meandering streams
'When absent ...': C.J.L. Price identifies this as Song VI of *Twelve Songs set to Music by William Jackson of Exeter: Opera Quarta* (n.d.). The first stanza runs:
When absent from my Soul's Delight,
What terrors fill my troubled Breast,
Once more return'd to thy lov'd sight,
Hope too returns, my fears have rest
'Go, gentle gales!': identified by C.J.L. Price as Song V from *Twelve Songs set to Music by William Jackson of Exeter*; the words are from Alexander Pope's 'Autumn: the third pastoral'

'My heart's my own ...': a song from Act I of *Love in a Village* (1762), a comic opera by Isaac Bickerstaff (1735–1812):

My heart's my own, my will is free,
And so shall be my voice;
No mortal man shall wed with me,
Till first he's made my choice

pipe:	the voice
catches and glees:	short songs, usually amusing, for three or more voices, without musical accompaniment
race ball:	an assembly for dancing at the time of some horse races
minuet:	a dance for two dancers, dignified, performed in short steps
country dancing:	generally danced boisterously
Od's swimmings:	God's swimmings; a swimming is a smooth, gliding movement of the body in dancing
Cotillon:	a lively dance for four or eight people. The word comes from the French, *cotillon*, a petticoat
monkey-led:	as if on a chain or lead
palming puppies:	a reference to dances where each lady gives her hand to each gentleman in turn, implying that the 'puppies' were keen to hold the ladies' hands
a managed filly:	a well trained young female horse, taught the *manège* of a riding school
the set:	the number of couples needed to perform a country dance
electrical:	the property of attracting light bodies when excited by friction; the state of excitation produced by friction or the exhalations which appear as sparks
looby:	a lout, fool
frogs:	ornamental fastening on the front of a coat
tambours:	embroidery frames
ancient madam:	Acres' mother
Od's triggers and flints:	a reference to duelling pistols: in the eighteenth century the gunpowder was ignited by sparks produced by the hammer of the pistol striking a flint
cashier:	get rid of, dismiss
incapable:	incapable of being worn any more, worn out
a new method of swearing:	see note on 'Od's whips and wheels!' above
militia:	a local force which could be raised by the Lords Lieutenant of a county in which citizens could be liable to have fourteen days' training in a year
sentiment:	opinion being expressed
genteel:	gentlemanly, suited to a gentleman

Jove: Jove, or Jupiter, King of the gods in classical mythology; the following gods and goddesses are also classical

Bacchus: the god of wine

Mars: the god of war

Venus: the goddess of love

Pallas: Pallas Athene, the Greek goddess of wisdom

oath ... echo to sense: this parodies a couplet in the *Essay on Criticism* (1711) by Alexander Pope (1688–1744)
> Tis not enough no harshness gives offence
> The sound must seem an echo to the sense

bumpers: cups or glasses filled to the brim; that is, he will drink her health with a full glass

gout: a painful swelling of the joints

pittance: a very small allowance

income ... commission: his warrant as an ensign; the income was probably nearly six shillings a day

live-stock: as opposed to dead stock (equipment, furniture), the animals, the living creatures on the estate

my vows are pledged: to pledge is to make something security for something borrowed

let her forclose: a legal term, from the law on mortgages; the lender of money can forclose if the money is not repaid within a certain time, forclosing meaning treating the pledge as his own property, refusing the borrower the right to redeem

the Crescent: the Royal Crescent, a street in Bath begun in 1767

Cox's Museum: James Cox opened an exhibition of mechanical toys and curiosities in the Spring Gardens, Bath, between 1772 and 1775

jackanapes: impertinent fellow

humour: mood

Z——ds!: Zounds! a corruption of 'God's wounds!'

lodge a five and three-pence: cut his son off with a quarter of a guinea

unget: unbeget

turnspit: the dog who turned a wheel in the kitchen which would in turn, through pulleys or shafts, turn the spit on which meat was roasted

triumvirate: a body composed of three men. The name arose from the Roman habit of calling commissions on public bodies by the number of men they contained, (thus, for instance, duumviri, a duumvirate or body of two men, triumviri, a body of three men). Here, 'puppy triumvirate' means an impertinent trio

Soh!:	So!
trims:	reprimands, scolds

Act 2 Scene 2

The scene is the North Parade, where Lucy, waiting for Sir Lucius, soliloquises, informing us that Captain Absolute is now another of the rivals for Lydia, that Acres has been dismissed, and that Sir Lucius expects a note from his Delia—she adds that he would not pay her so well if he knew Delia was nearly fifty and her own mistress. When Sir Lucius does arrive he reads the letter; he thinks that he is involved with Lydia, and that they must get the aunt's consent to their marriage.

Sir Lucius leaves and Fag enters; he has seen Lucy giving Sir Lucius a letter and says he'll tell his master. Lucy assures him that the letter was from Mrs Malaprop, and that his master (Beverley) has a rival, now that Sir Anthony has proposed his son as a suitor.

NOTES AND GLOSSARY:

until my purse has received notice:	until I've been sufficiently bribed
dear Dalia:	she is mocking the Irish accent of Sir Lucius O'Trigger
South Parade:	in Bath
North:	the North Parade in Bath
Coffee-house:	Coffee-houses were houses of entertainment where coffee and other refreshments were provided; they were very popular in the seventeenth and eighteenth century, probably as venues for political and literary conversation
induction:	the letter is from Mrs Malaprop. She probably means here 'production' or 'seduction'
commotion:	perhaps 'emotion'
superfluous:	superficial
punctuation:	punctilio, punctiliousness
infallible:	perhaps 'ineffable'
pressed:	impressed; the image is of people forced by the Press Gang into the armed services
habeas-corpus:	(*Latin*) 'you may have the body'; a writ of *habeas corpus* requires that someone detained should be brought before a judge, and thus protects a person from imprisonment without trial
the old gentlewoman:	he means Mrs Malaprop
nice:	particular, scrupulous
gemman:	gentleman. Lucy is pretending to be simple
pho:	an exclamation

baggage:	cheeky, saucy girl
call him out:	challenge him to a duel
address:	bearing, attitude

Act 3 Scene 1

The scene is again the North Parade, where Captain Absolute finds Fag's news amusing, that Sir Anthony wants to force him to marry the girl with whom he is plotting to run away. When his father enters, he tells him that he has decided to sacrifice his own inclinations to Sir Anthony's satisfaction. He pretends to remember neither Mrs Malaprop nor Lydia. He pretends also to an indifference which makes his father think him phlegmatic. He charges Jack with being a hypocrite, but his son says solemnly that he is sorry that his father should so mistake the respect and duty he bears to him. On this Sir Anthony says he'll arrange for Jack to visit Lydia at once.

NOTES AND GLOSSARY:

getting:	begetting
marching regiment:	one without settled quarters, liable to be sent anywhere
condescension:	affability, kindness
neck:	here, the exposed upper part of a woman's body
Od's life:	God's life
phlegmatic:	cold, dull, sluggish. Apathy was thought to be caused by possession of phlegm, one of the four humours of old physiology
anchorite:	a hermit, a recluse who shuts himself off from the world
stock:	a stupid, lethargic person
a block ... regimentals:	a block was a piece of wood on which regimentals (uniforms) were placed so that they could be beaten to free them of dust
Promethean torch:	in classical mythology Prometheus made man out of clay and lit his torch at the chariot of the sun, bringing fire to man, and thus enabling him to master nature. Lydia's eyes will put life into Jack

---

Act 3 Scene 2

This scene, between Faulkland and Julia, satirises excessive sensibility. Faulkland's high-flown speech expresses his self-regarding jealousy; he taxes Julia with her enjoying life in his absence. Julia has missed him, however, and tells him she has pretended to be happy so that her friends should not guess his unkindness had caused her tears. Faulkland then fears she is grateful to him rather than loving him. He goes on until she leaves in tears. Then he is sorry for quarrelling with her and decides not to risk upsetting her again.

NOTES AND GLOSSARY:

veering but a point: one of the thirty-two points of the mariner's compass, each equalling 11°15′
title: claim
person: personal appearance, good looks
this **vain article:** this trifling matter (of personal appearance)
Æthiop: an Ethiopian
contract: a contract to marry
S'death: euphemistic abbreviation of 'God's death'
virago: noisy, bad-tempered woman

Act 3 Scene 3

The scene is set in Mrs Malaprop's lodgings where she is receiving Captain Absolute. He compliments her, and tells her he is not prejudiced against Lydia for having involved herself with Ensign Beverley. Mrs Malaprop says she has intercepted another note from Beverley. Absolute realises this is the note he had given to Lucy earlier; he reads the letter aloud: in it Beverley had written that his new rival Absolute had 'the character of being an accomplished gentleman and a man of honour' (thus Absolute had been laying the ground for later revealing his true identity to Lucy), had abused Mrs Malaprop for her vanity, her misuse of language and her openness to flattery, and had assured Lydia that he hoped to make Mrs Malaprop a go-between for an interview with her.

Absolute then suggests that Mrs Malaprop should allow Lydia to correspond with Beverley, even let her plot an elopement, while he will have Beverley laid by the heels and carry off Lydia himself. Mrs Malaprop agrees, and then goes off to bring Lydia to meet Captain Absolute. He thinks that though he could now abandon his disguise he would probably lose Lydia, through her caprice. When Lydia comes in, and realises Beverley is there, he explains that he has deceived Mrs Malaprop, passing himself off on her as Captain Absolute. He proposes to her, asks her to run away with him, but when Mrs Malaprop comes in Lydia seems, to her, to be cold to the Captain, saying that though her aunt's choice may be Absolute, hers is Beverley. Absolute, finding Mrs Malaprop still thinks him to be Absolute, tells her that time will bring Lydia round. There follows some very amusing conversation with double meanings, where both Mrs Malaprop and Lydia expose their ignorance of the true situation: Lydia denies having told Absolute she loves another man better and Mrs Malaprop charges her with having boasted that Beverley possessed her heart, to which Lydia assents—on which they all leave, with Lydia calling for blessings on Beverley, and Absolute kissing his hand to her.

NOTES AND GLOSSARY:

accommodation:	recommendation
ingenuity:	ingenuousness
ineffectual:	intellectual
orange-tree:	on which fruit and flowers can appear together
pine-apple:	pinnacle
strolling:	tramping
exploded:	exposed
conjunctions:	injunctions
preposition:	proposition
enjoin:	enforce upon
particle:	article
hydrostatics:	hysterics
persisted:	desisted
reprehend:	apprehend or comprehend
oracular:	vernacular
derangement:	arrangement
epitaphs:	epithets
hanged and quartered:	cut up into four pieces after being hanged, a traitor's execution
coxcomb:	a conceited, impertinent person; the term comes from the cock's comb on a jester's cap
harridan's:	ill-tempered old woman's
in the nick:	in the nick of time, just in time
laid by the heels:	captured and confined
licensed warmth:	he proposes to elope with her and marry her, hence licensed means, here, married or permitted
antipodes:	places on the opposite side of the world
vixen:	term of abuse, a she-fox
an allegory:	an alligator
stroller:	a vagabond, a tramp, or an itinerant actor

Act 3 Scene 4

In Acres' lodgings Acres is told by his servant David how different he is as a result of his new style of dressing. David leaves and Acres practices some dancing steps; he is visited by Sir Lucius O'Trigger, who asks the reason for his visiting Bath. When Acres tells him that he has come to

Bath and heard that the young lady he is in love with has another lover, Beverley, Sir Lucius tells him that if he thinks he has been supplanted unfairly he must fight this man who has dared to fall in love with the same woman. Acres argues that he does not know Beverley, but Sir Lucius urges him on, and Acres writes a formal letter at his dictation, asking Beverley to meet him at King's Mead Fields to settle the matter. Sir Lucius suggests the meeting should take place as soon as possible, that evening; he regrets he cannot act as second to Acres, but he himself has another similar affair on his hands, with 'a gay captain here who put a jest' on him lately, whom he is seeking to challenge to a duel.

NOTES AND GLOSSARY:

monkeyrony ... printshops: a corruption of 'macaroni', a term used at the time, as was 'monkey' for a dandy. Caricatures of well known macaronis (who affected Italian fashions) were for sale in print shops (shops which sold portraits, caricatures and views)

Clod Hall: Bob Acres' home in Devonshire, in the south-west of England

Lard presarve me: Lord preserve me

Dolly Tester: a tester-bed was one with a canopy, hence Dolly was a chambermaid

oons: the same as 'zounds'

I'll hold a gallon ... but would bark: I'll bet a gallon that the dogs won't know you

De-la-Grace: he is a French dancing master

balancing ... chasing ... boring: terms used in dancing, from the French *balancer, chasser, faire le pas bourrée*. The *bourrée* was danced frequently in Auvergne, in France, and was a very lively dance

Sink, glide—coupee: more terms used in dancing

Od's jigs and tabors: another 'oath referential': tabors are small drums

valued: took seriously

cross-over to couple ... figure in ...: a term used in country dancing

allemandes: a lively German dance, so called from the French word for 'German'

lingo: (*slang*) language

pas: (*French*) step

anti-gallican: opposed to what is French

Cupid's Jack-a-lantern ... quagmire: Cupid was the god of love in classical mythology; a jack-a-lantern *ignis fatuus*, the will-o'-the-wisp, a flame caused by marsh gas, which deceives travellers, leading them on to boggy ground

We wear no swords here: Beau Nash had forbodden the wearing of swords in Bath, because they tore the ladies' clothes

Gad: God

Achilles: the Greek warrior in Homer's *Iliad*

little: term of affection

Alexander the Great: King of Macedonia (356–323BC) who by conquest extended his Empire into India

grenadier's march: this, a well known song, begins 'some talk of Alexander and some of Achilles'

pans: the part of the lock of a gun or pistol which held the gunpowder

Blunderbuss-Hall: Sir Lucius O'Trigger's home

view room: the upper assembly rooms east of the Circus at Bath; they were opened in 1771

the milk of human kindness: from Shakespeare's *Macbeth*, I, 5:

> Yet do I fear thy nature
> It is too full of the milk of human kindness
> To catch the nearest way

'I could do such deeds': here Acres may be thinking of a passage in Shakespeare's *King Lear*, II, 4:

> I will do such things—
> What they are, yet I know not, but they shall be
> The terrors of the earth

Indite: set down in writing

damme: short form of damn me, here a noun, the name of the oath

King's Mead Fields: land on the west side of Bath, originally part of the King's demesne and then a rendezvous for public breakfasts, teas, and concerts

---

Act 4 Scene 1

This scene also takes place in Acres' lodgings, and also opens with talk between Acres and David. David takes a realistic view of duelling, but Acres is concerned about his honour, about disgracing his ancestors. David thinks the odds are ten to one against his master, but Acres says he will not be put off by him. David leaves when Captain Absolute arrives, and is asked by Acres to deliver a challenge to Beverley; he says that he will see that Beverley receives it, but that he cannot with propriety act as Acres' second. Acres suggests that Absolute should tell Beverley that Acres is a determined duellist, and kills a man a week, and Absolute, in leaving, assures him that he will describe him as '*Fighting Bob*'.

NOTES AND GLOSSARY:

cormorants: sea birds proverbially considered voracious

quarter-staff: a long pole, from six to eight feet long, tipped with metal

short staff: a cudgel

sharps and snaps: duelling swords and pistols

the profit of it: the speech is reminiscent of Falstaff's realistic comments on honour in Shakespeare's *1 Henry IV*, V, 1

I go to the worms: I am buried

poltroon: spiritless coward

Crop: Acres' horse

St George and the dragon: St George, a saint martyed in the reign of Diocletian, was adopted as the patron saint of England from the time of Edward III. The jewel of the order of St George shows the saint encountering the dragon

raven: ravens were considered birds of ill omen

proper: because Absolute is supposed to be Beverley's friend

Act 4 Scene 2

This scene, in many respects the turning-point of the play, takes place in Mrs Malaprop's lodgings. Mrs Malaprop praises Captain Absolute to Lydia, who, in an aside, forecasts Mrs Malaprop's rage when she discovers that Absolute is Lydia's Beverley. When Sir Anthony and Captain Absolute are announced Lydia says she will not even speak to or look at the Captain.

Sir Anthony urges Jack to speak to Lydia but he begs his father to leave him alone with Lydia. Lydia is waiting for her aunt to discover that the Captain is not the man who called on them earlier. Both Sir Anthony and Mrs Malaprop urge the young people to speak to each other. Jack speaks in a low, hoarse voice hoping that Lydia will not recognise it and look round. Lydia recognises Beverley and after some moments of disbelief Sir Anthony realises he has been taken in. Lydia is furious that there will be no elopement and it dawns on Mrs Malaprop that Beverley's letters were written by Absolute. Sir Anthony suggests to Mrs Malaprop that they should forgive the young people, and they leave Absolute and Lydia to sort matters out.

At first Lydia is cool, and then furious that Jack has been humouring her romance, treating her like a child. It looks as if Lydia may forgive him but then she bursts into tears as Sir Anthony and Mrs Malaprop reappear. They are baffled by this but, on Lydia's flouncing out, saying that she renounces him for ever, Jack is taxed by his father with having been over-eager and frightening Lydia, which Jack denies. However, Sir Anthony says that Mrs Malaprop must make his peace for him.

NOTES AND GLOSSARY:

caparisons:	comparisons. Caparisons are trappings for horses
physiognomy:	phraseology
Hamlet says:	from Shakespeare's *Hamlet* III, 4:

> Hyperion's curls; the front of Jove himself;
> An eye to Mars, to threaten and command;
> A station like the herald Mercury
> New-lighted on a heaven-kissing hill

Hyperion, in classical mythology, was the father of the sun and moon. Station means posture

similitude:	simile
affluence:	influence
quinsy:	inflammation of the throat or part of it, tonsilitis
Bedlam:	the hospital of St Mary of Bethlehem, originally a priory. It was given to the City of London in 1547 and then converted into a lunatic asylum. It was close to Moorfields
compilation:	appellation
clever:	neat
anticipate:	exacerbate
retrospection:	introspection. Mrs Malaprop is mixing herself thoroughly in saying they will not foresee the past and look back on the future
Youth's the season:	a song from *The Beggar's Opera* (1728) by John Gay (1685–1732):

> Youth's the season made for joys,
> Love is then our duty;
> She alone who that employs
> Well deserves her beauty.
> Let's be gay,
> While we may,
> Beauty's a flower, despised in decay ...

analysed:	paralysed
Cerberus:	in classical mythology, the three-headed dog of Pluto, which guarded the entrance to Hades

Act 4 Scene 3

Sir Lucius is walking on the North Parade seeking Captain Absolute, who enters in a thoroughly bad humour as his schemes have gone wrong.

Sir Lucius quarrels with him, asking to name his time and place; and Absolute replies the sooner the better, naming the Spring Gardens, that evening. Sir Lucius suggests King's Mead Fields instead, at about six o'clock, to which Absolute agrees. After Sir Lucius leaves Faulkland enters, to be told of Lydia's change of mind and of Sir Lucius's challenge, and asks to act as Absolute's second. Faulkland informs Absolute of his own quarrel with Julia, blaming his own 'vile tormenting temper' for it. A letter from Julia is brought by a servant. In this she forgives Faulkland and tells him she wishes to speak with him as soon as possible. Faulkland then begins to wonder whether Julia is indelicate in her quick forgiveness of him. Absolute, leaving, has no patience with him, thinking him more fit for ridicule than compassion. Faulkland then thinks he will use his involvement in the duel as a means of testing Julia's sincerity once and for all.

NOTES AND GLOSSARY:

the old serpent: the tempter in the Garden of Eden (see the Bible, Genesis 3)

vipers ... red cloth: red cloth was said to attract vipers; similarly soldiers, known from their uniforms as redcoats, attracted women. Vipers wasted their venom on the cloth and could then be picked up without danger

gypsy: cheat

balk: disappoint, frustrate

pother: fuss, commotion

name your time and place: a formula used in issuing a challenge to a duel

Spring Gardens: on the Bathwick side of Pulteney Bridge, a place where public breakfasts, concerts and firework displays were held

small-sword: a duelling sword or rapier for thrusting

swivel: since he talks of Lydia's eye securing a retreat this may be a military echo in Absolute's speech, a swivel being a pivoted rest for a gun

not unsought be won: from *Paradise Lost* (1667) VIII, 502–3 by John Milton (1608–74):
Her virtue, and the conscience of her worth
That would be wooed, and not unsought be won

touchstone: a black stone of quartz or jasper, used for testing the purity of gold or silver, hence that which serves to test the genuineness of anything

sterling: genuine, pure, of true worth (of money, conforming to the national standard of value)

allay: alloy

Act 5 Scene 1

This scene is set in Julia's dressing-room. Julia has been upset by a message from Faulkland, who comes in to take, he says, a long farewell. He tells her he has to fly from the Kingdom immediately, and wishes he had married her before this mischance. Julia replies that she will fly with him; he suggests she should take time to think this over, but she says that in the event of his fortune being forfeited she has enough for them to live on. He is worried that he might be an unpleasant person to live with, his wounded pride affecting his fretful temper, to which she replies that he will the more need some affectionate person to console him. At this he reveals that he has pretended the whole thing, but asks her to forgive him and marry him next day. Julia rejoices that he is free from crime but tells him how his cruel doubts have wrung her heart, accusing him of trifling with her sincerity. After a year of trial, she thinks he will never change his nature, and, while she will never change her love for him, asks that it should not be the least of his regrets that he has lost the love of someone who would have followed him in beggary through the world.

When she goes Faulkland realises what he has done, and what he has lost in Julia; he leaves for the duel. Lydia comes in and is joined by Julia, who does not say why she has been crying. Lydia finds that Julia knew who Beverley was; she expresses her disappointment at the idea of marriage instead of an elopement and recalls the stratagems in which she had to indulge to have a few moments' conversation with her love. Julia urges her not to let her caprice ruin Absolute's happiness.

At this point Mrs Malaprop, Fag and David enter, and Fag tells the girls what he has already explained to Mrs Malaprop, that Captain Absolute is involved in a duel. David adds that Acres and Faulkland are also implicated in it, as well as Sir Lucius O'Trigger. Mrs Malaprop urges them to go to the place of assignment to prevent mischief. David is sent to look for Sir Anthony, and the others, under Fag's guidance, seek the duellists.

NOTES AND GLOSSARY:

licensed power: position as her husband (the reference is to a marriage licence)

influence, like the moon's ... madness: a reference to the belief that madness was caused by the influence of the moon (in Latin, *luna*, hence 'lunatic')

Smithfield bargain: Smithfield was the main London cattle-market; she means a marriage where money is the main concern

Scotch parson: eloping couples frequently went to Scotland where, unlike the legal position in England, minors could marry without the consent of parents or guardians

flimsy:	paltry, insignificant
bishop's licence:	a bishop can grant a licence for a couple to marry in a church where one of them resides (thus avoiding the reading of banns)
cried three times:	the banns are read on three successive occasions in the church; they provide public notice of a marriage, so that those who know of any impediment to it can lodge objections
O lud!:	O Lord!
paracide:	parricide: the murder of one's father (or a near relation)
Simulation:	dissimulation
antistrophe:	catastrophe
enveloped:	developed (or, perhaps, divulged)
flourishing:	developing the subject in a flowery manner
perpendiculars:	particulars
fire-office:	insurance company's office dealing with fires
angry favour:	inflamed appearance (as of a wound)
participate:	precipitate
Derbyshire petrifactions:	the Peak District in Derbyshire, with caves where there are stalactites and stalagmites (a stalactite is an icicle-like formation hanging from the roof or sides of a cavern, it is formed of calcium carbonate by the dropping of water percolating through and partially dissolving the overlying limestone; a stalagmite is a deposit on the floor of a cavern)
felicity:	velocity
exhort:	escort
envoy:	perhaps convoy, the equivalent of an escort or guide
precede:	proceed

Act 5 Scene 2

Captain Absolute, hiding his sword under his greatcoat, is on the South Parade; he tries to evade his father, pretending to be someone else, then he tells him it was a joke. Sir Anthony discovers the concealed sword, but his son explains that he intends, if Lydia will not forgive him, to threaten to fall on it and die at her feet. Sir Anthony thinks this may be the very thing that will please her, and the Captain leaves him, just before Acres' servant David appears, running and bawling, urging Sir Anthony to stop the captain. He explains that there is to be fighting at King's Mead Fields. Sir Anthony and he leave at once.

NOTES AND GLOSSARY:

Sword seen ... in Bath: both parties in duels were arrested in Bath, on Beau Nash's orders

beadles: parish officers who kept order in church, acted as general parish servants and punished offenders

shoulder: he has the gout, and needs to lean on David

Act 5 Scene 3

Acres and Sir Lucius are at King's Mead Fields, Sir Lucius measuring out a short distance, while Acres argues in favour of forty yards between the opponents, to Sir Lucius's scorn. Sir Lucius asks if he can do anything for him 'in case of an accident', and gives him advice on how to stand. When Sir Lucius sees two men coming over a stile Acres becomes very worried and feels his valour ebbing rapidly.

At this point Faulkland and Captain Absolute reach them. Sir Lucius assumes Absolute has come to second his friend and then fight his own duel; he thinks Faulkland is Beverley. Acres explains to Sir Lucius that Absolute and Faulkland are his friends. Sir Lucius thinks that since Acres challenged somebody and came to fight him, then if one of his two friends represents Beverley, it will be all right. Absolute explains that he is Beverley, and Acres says he would never quarrel with his friend. After some argument with Acres Sir Lucius decides it is time he and Absolute began. They have just drawn their swords, when Sir Anthony, David and the women arrive. Sir Anthony demands reasons for the duel and his son explains that Sir Lucius has called him out without explaining his reasons. Mrs Malaprop interrupts the men, telling Absolute that Lydia has been terrified on his account. Lydia then says she wants to marry Absolute, who tells Sir Lucius there must be some mistake, for he has never intended to affront him. Sir Lucius accepts his apology, but takes out his letters from Delia, asking Lydia if she is his Delia or not. Mrs Malaprop admits that she herself is Delia, but Sir Lucius finds this hard to believe, and says to Absolute that since he has taken Lydia from him he'll give him Delia into the bargain. Absolute says that Acres is not yet settled, but he withdraws, and makes his peace with Sir Lucius. They all retire, while Julia yet again forgives Faulkland. Sir Anthony urges Julia to marry him directly, saying that Faulkland's faults proceed from his affection for Julia. Sir Lucius, though disappointed, takes pleasure in seeing others succeed, and Bob Acres shows he is neither vexed nor angry by bidding them all to a party in the New Rooms in half an hour. Faulkland acknowledges the power of their ladies in reforming them, Absolute teases him for having created his own troubles, and Lydia says she prepared Jack's for him. But, she says, our happiness is now general, a point taken up finally by Julia who offers advice on how to keep it so.

NOTES AND GLOSSARY:

musket:	a handgun used by infantry. It would carry far further than a pistol
field pieces:	artillery which can be moved
Pho!:	an exclamation
be easy:	don't be sought after
Quietus:	death (from the Latin, *quietus est*, he is quit of his incumbrances, figuratively, is dead). Here used as in Shakespeare's *Hamlet* III, 1:
	For who would bear the whips and scorns of time ...
	When he himself might his quietus make
	With a bare bodkin
pickled:	a way of preserving bodies
the Abbey:	the Abbey Church at Bath
files:	swords without edges, used in fencing
cocked:	ready to fire, with the lever in the gun raised ready to be released by the trigger
of its own head:	of its own accord
as lieve:	just as soon, just as gladly
backs and abettors:	backers (supporters) and helpers
poltroon:	spiritless coward
counsellor:	lawyer, barrister. He means Acres is more ready to argue than fight
I serve his Majesty:	as an army officer, Absolute could not refuse a challenge
brook:	accept, tolerate
delusions:	allusions
dissolve:	solve or resolve
Impeachment:	reproach
Vandyke:	Vandal. The Vandals, a Teutonic tribe, plundered Rome in the fifth century and were known for their barbarity; the word came to mean any wilful destroyer. Van Dyck (1599–1641) was a Flemish artist patronised by Charles I
condescension:	kindness to an inferior. Sir Lucius is being ironic
we single lads:	Sir Anthony is a widower

Epilogue

The speaker says that the poet (Sheridan) said he would try to coax a moral from the play, but she argues that one moral is clear: man's social happiness depends on women. Both love and women are essential in drama—and in life. She lists the citizen, the surly squire, the jolly toper and statesmen as ruled by women's influence, and says the same is true in humbler life, citing the peasant, the sailor and the soldier. Then she says some cautious people think judgement must fix the darts that Beauty throws. But, she argues, if sense and merit ruled women's feelings, then lovers' minds would accept their teaching and beaux would light the lamp of knowledge from the torch of love. It is a light, ironic piece of verse.

NOTES AND GLOSSARY:

damned: a reference to a play which did not succeed at its first performance

The cit: the citizen, meaning middle-class merchants

John Trot: proverbial name for an uncultivated person in the eighteenth century

vanquished victor: from *Alexander's Feast* by John Dryden (1631–1700):

> At length with love and wine at once oppress'd
> The vanquish'd victor sunk upon her breast.

Toper: drinker

tardy blade: this could mean that the jolly toper reproaches those of his companions (blade, a lively, cheery fellow) for drinking too slowly (but C.J. Price in his edition of 1968 explains blade as a blade of corn, especially malting barley)

Chloe: a name used by love poets, particularly in the eighteenth century

tar: sailor

Susan: the reference is to a ballad by John Gay (1685–1732) called 'Sweet William's Farewell to Black-eyed Susan'

fairly: justly

Nancy: another conventional name, usually given to soldiers' girls

beaux: lovers, dandies, fine gentlemen

Gallantry: love. The beaux show their gallantry in love as soldiers do on the field of war

Part 3

Commentary

IN THE COMEDY OF MANNERS characters are not usually deeply developed; society itself is mildly ridiculed and deviations from the norm are mocked; amusemment is also produced by situations into which characters get themselves.

The characters

Sir Anthony Absolute

Sir Anthony is a widower, a crusty, conservative and wealthy baronet. He is a man of sudden whims, and accustomed to having his own way. He answers Mrs Malaprop, who asks him if his son Jack will have any objection to marrying Lydia, 'Objection!—let him object if he dare!' The slightest demur puts him in a frenzy; indeed he is perpetually warning people not to put him in one. He is opinionated; he has earlier denounced circulating libraries, and is against teaching girls to read. Later he advises Mrs Malaprop to keep Lydia under lock and key if she rejects the idea of marrying Jack, and adds 'If you were just to let the servants forget to bring her dinner for three or four days, you can't conceive how she'd come about'.

When Sir Anthony meets his son he tells him how he has resolved to fix him 'at once in a noble independence' by arranging for him to marry a wealthy wife. He refuses to inform Jack who the lady is, and when Jack says his heart is engaged to another, he tells his son not to put him in a frenzy. He works himself into one in a moment, threatening to disown and disinherit his son if he does not agree to do everything he chooses.

In the third act he begins to carry out his threats, only to find Jack agreeing to his plans. He is disappointed at Jack's reception of his news that the girl is 'blooming love-breathing seventeen'. And he finally denounces Jack as a phlegmatic sot, when Jack delivers a solemn speech asserting that all he desires in the matter is to please his father.

He brings Jack to pay his respects to Mrs Malaprop and Lydia Languish in the fourth act, and is peremptory when Jack is silent: 'Why don't you begin, Jack?—Speak, you puppy—Speak!' When Jack eventually talks to Lydia and is called Beverley by her, Sir Anthony is baffled at first, but he does realise—more quickly than Mrs Malaprop—

what has been happening. After a certain amount of expostulation, however, he decides to forget and forgive, and persuades Mrs Malaprop to do the same. He is greatly cheered by the prospect of Jack and Lydia in love. But when he and Mrs Malaprop return, having left the stage to the young couple for a time, he is amazed by the fact that they have obviously been quarrelling: 'What the devil's the matter now! Zounds! Mrs Malaprop, this is the *oddest billing* and *cooing* I ever heard!' He finally assumes Jack has been too lively and frightened Lydia. And in his genial way, after Lydia has left, renouncing Beverley for ever, he assures Jack that Mrs Malaprop will make his peace. He is, in fact, pleased that Jack is impatient, and 'a young villain'.

In the fifth act when Sir Anthony meets Jack in the street he eventually sends him off to Lydia with an amiable dismissal: 'Get along—and damn your trinkets'. Having learned that Jack's sword was really being concealed because his son was bound for a duel, he again announces he will be in a frenzy, as he dashes off, supported by Acres' servant David, to stop the duel.

He interrupts the preliminaries of the duel, and then supports Jack in asserting his claims to Lydia, comforts Mrs Malaprop after Sir Lucius has declared his lack of interest in her, and then makes peace between Julia and Faulkland. He conveys his basic amiability in his final remarks: 'Gad! Sir, I like your spirit; and at night we single lads will drink a health to the young couples, and a husband to Mrs Malaprop.' In general, beneath his blustering, hectoring manner (for which his gout may provide some excuse), Sir Anthony eventually seems to have a certain benignity.

Captain Jack Absolute

Jack Absolute is in love with Lydia Languish. To humour her romantic ideas about love and marriage he pretends to be an ensign on half pay, calling himself Beverley, so that she will not realise he is the son and heir of the well-to-do Sir Anthony Absolute. He is not willing to persuade her to run away with him; he wants to prepare her gradually for the discovery of his real identity, because he is afraid she will not agree to the 'impediment of our friends' consent, a regular humdrum wedding, and the reversion of a good fortune on my side'. He sees himself as a romantic lover, but certainly not in the way that Faulkland is one: indeed he teases Faulkland for being stupidly jealous. He is courteous and polite; for instance, he receives Bob Acres' new way of wearing his hair, dressing and swearing tolerantly without mocking him as he might well have.

His relationship with his father is amusing and skilfully handled by Sheridan. Jack is polite to his father, even though Sir Anthony has suddenly announced that he has chosen his bride for him and will not even tell him who she is. Jack's firm insistence that he has pledged his vows to another provokes a violent outburst from Sir Anthony. The quarrel between father and son is part and parcel of the tradition of the comedy of manners. Sir Anthony sees himself as 'compliance itself'— when he gets his own way. And there is humour in the way the father attacks his son for being passionate and sneering. When Sir Anthony leaves, Jack muses on the fact that his father had himself been a bold intriguer in his youth and married for love.

When Jack realises that his father wants to force him to marry the girl with whom he is actually planning to run away, he decides to recant and appear pentitential. He does this to such an extent that his father gets irritated with him for being so indifferent to his descriptions of Lydia's charms. He even asks if his father intends him to marry the aunt or the niece, and when his father erupts at this ('The *aunt* indeed!—Od's life! When I ran away with your mother I would not have touched anything old or ugly to gain an empire') he permits himself the ironic query, 'not to please your father, sir?' Sir Anthony has to backtrack rather rapidly! Eventually Jack's acting is so convincing that Sir Anthony thinks him either a 'phlegmatic sot' or a hypocrite. But, even so, he cannot provoke Jack into saying that he is activated other than by respect and duty.

When he calls on Mrs Malaprop there is a good deal of comic irony about the scene, since the audience knows more about the situation than Mrs Malaprop. Jack's reading aloud, at Mrs Malaprop's instigation, Ensign Beverley's letter (this is the letter which he has written to Lydia), with its sharp reflections on Mrs Malaprop, is funny, and his quick lover's invention is apparent when he suggests that Mrs Malaprop should let Lydia plot an elopement with Beverley so that he (as Absolute) can carry her off instead. And then he is quick to tell Lydia how he has pretended to be Absolute: and he can launch himself into the high-flown romantic nonsense Lydia obviously likes so much. Jack is also quick in covering up Lydia's protestations that only Beverley possesses her heart when Mrs Malaprop returns.

Jack enjoys his double identity—for instance, he uses double meanings effectively when he tells Acres that Beverley will get the challenge Acres has asked Jack to deliver. But he cannot manage to keep up his deception when Sir Anthony and he call on Mrs Malaprop and Lydia together. While he wins over his father by revealing his role as Beverley he also runs the risk of losing Lydia's love. And in this mood of anger he accepts Sir Lucius's challenge with dignity even though he is entirely unaware of having affronted him. In his own despair—'disappointed by other people's folly'—he still urges Faulkland to be sensible about Julia, sensibly regarding him as more fit for ridicule than compassion, since he is creating his own troubles.

Absolute's quick invention appears yet again when, en route to his duel with Sir Lucius, he meets his father and hides from him the true reason for his having a sword concealed under his coat: once arrived at King's Mead Fields he has to explain to Bob Acres that he is Beverley, but, once that quarrel is settled, he still has to fight Sir Lucius. He has been ready to fight them both because his love for Lydia is the real reason for the quarrels. He explains to his father when Sir Anthony arrives that, as an army officer, he could not refuse Sir Lucius's challenge—and, once Lydia forgives him, he continues resolutely to say he will support his claim to her against any man. He is courageous enough to apologise to Sir Lucius for any affront he might inadvertently have given him. (This was a difficult thing to do, in days when 'honour' was at stake in matters of challenges, and it required common sense and equanimity of character to make an apology without incurring the risk of seeming cowardly or lacking in 'honour'.) And so, in the end, he gains his love.

Faulkland

Faulkland is a character who is perhaps a little difficult for a modern audience or modern readers to fathom fully. In him Sheridan is mocking the current vogue for sentimentality. Faulkland was appreciated by contemporary audiences—and by Julia, who thinks he is 'too proud, too noble to be jealous'. She is wrong in this, as it turns out, for, as Jack Absolute remarks to Acres, Faulkland *is* 'a little jealous'. But then Julia and Faulkland are in love with each other. She thinks his affection is 'ardent and sincere'; he tells Absolute that he has 'set his happiness on this cast, and not to succeed, were to be stripped of all'. He is over sensitive; he fears for 'her spirits—her health—her life'. But after he tells Jack Absolute that he would be 'happy beyond measure' if he knew Julia were well and cheerful, he is soon upset by this very news, given by Acres, that Julia is well, is lively and entertaining, so full of wit and humour. He thinks Julia has not been thinking of him while they have been apart and works himself into a rage, thinking that while he has been 'anxious, silent, pensive, sedentary' she has been 'all health! spirit! laugh! song! dance!' He is furious because she has been singing, and singing cheerful songs at that, and because she has been dancing.

Faulkland, however, knows in his heart how silly he is. Waiting for Julia, in Act 3 Scene 2, he thinks that he is captious and capricious. Yet when she arrives he taxes her with her high spirits in Devonshire; he would regard every mirthful moment he might have had in her absence 'as a treason to constancy'. He finally upsets her so much that she leaves in tears, and after waiting in vain for her to return, he decides never to distress her again. He is hard to please: when she writes to him, he is afraid to open the letter in case she is dismissing him; but when Jack Absolute reads it and Faulkland finds that Julia is not upbraiding him for his behaviour but forgiving him, he again finds fault with her. Jack Absolute has no patience with him, calling him a 'captious sceptic in love, a slave to fretfulness and whim', and Faulkland decides to make a final test of Julia's sincerity.

His plan, as he enacts it in the first scene of Act 5, is to tell Julia that he must fly the country because of a quarrel. When she offers to run away with him and marry him when they are safe from pursuit, and, despite his demurring, insists on accompanying him, he tells her that he has pretended to being involved in a crime in order to test her. She tells him that he has lost her love and leaves: whereupon he laments his 'cursed folly'.

When Julia discovers that he was involved in the plans for duelling at King's Mead Fields she forgives him, and he realises he will be 'blessed indeed'; her gentleness and candour have reformed his 'unhappy temper'.

However tiresome and finicky Faulkland may seem to us, he obviously is capable of suffering, and, though he has only himself to blame for that suffering, he is not an unreal character. Indeed, the character of Faulkland appeared to 'A friend to comedy', writing in the *Morning Chronicle and London Advertiser* of 20 January 1775, to be 'touched with a delicate and masterly hand', and to another writer in the *Morning Post*, four days later, to have 'exquisite refinement'. Where we may find the scenes with Faulkland excessively artificial we must remember that the audience of Sheridan's day could find them affecting.

Acres

Bob Acres is a good-hearted fellow. He tries hard to invest his language with liveliness. Indeed his first speech in Act 2 Scene 1 describing his having travelled like a comet with a trail of dust at his heels excited the condemnation of *Public Ledger*, of 18 January 1775, when it commented on Sheridan's using 'puns, witticisms, similes and metaphors' as substitutes for 'polished diction'. But Acres explains his new method of swearing to Jack Absolute, the *oath referential*, or sentimental swearing, and Jack calls it very genteel and very new.

Acres hopes that he will make a better impression on Lydia by dressing well and getting rid of his country clothes (there is a hint that his mother—'ancient madam'—has chosen his clothes for him). In Act 3 Scene 4 we see him practising his dancing steps, and his servant David has been reminding him of his background. When he meets Sir Lucius and tells him that he has heard Lydia is to be married to someone else, Sir Lucius tells him what has to be done. Acres resists the idea at first, then says courage must be catching and decides to challenge Beverley. He works himself into a passion, and Sir Lucius instructs him on how to write a civil challenge. In the next scene, the first of Act 4, Acres, in response to his servant David's querying the need for fighting, replies that his honour is involved. Acres is disturbed by David's comments on the dangers of duelling and the uselessness of honour once one is in the grave. None the less he sends the challenge to Beverley via Jack Absolute, whom he asks to describe him (to Beverley) as a devil of a fellow, a fighting man. Acres obviously hopes to avoid the duel if he clears his honour, though he says he wants to avoid taking Beverley's life.

When Acres comes to King's Mead Fields, in Act 5 Scene 3, he is obviously worried, and is all for placing a large distance—'forty or eight and thirty yards'—between himself and the other duellist. He shows his fears once Faulkland and Absolute appear, and when Absolute reveals that he is Beverley immediately says there is no quarrel involved. When Sir Lucius tells him he is little better than a coward he resents it, but gets out of any argument quickly. His good humour emerges at the end of the play. He shakes hands with Sir Lucius and shortly afterwards announces that he will give a party for everyone at the New Rooms in half an hour to show that he is 'neither vexed nor angry'.

Acres is a country squire: he lacks the poise of Absolute and the excessive refinement of Faulkland, and he verges on the ridiculous in his sampling of life in Bath, though he does try to maintain his concept of honour. His use of language is lively in the extreme, and he obviously has a peaceful, pleasant life at his home in Devonshire.

Sir Lucius O'Trigger

Sir Lucius O'Trigger's part was rewritten by Sheridan after the first performance of the play. The role was acted badly by Lee, who adopted 'a horrid medley of discordant brogues' according to the *Public Ledger* of 18 January 1795. By 30 January following, the improvement of the part by Sheridan was recorded by the *Morning Chronicle and London Advertiser*, the sentiments thrown into the mouth of Sir Lucius O'Trigger now producing 'a good effect, at the same time that they take away every possible idea of the characters being designed as an insult to our neighbours on the other side of St George's Channel' (the Irish). Sheridan had made Sir Lucius less of a stage Irishman in his revisions, and the part was played by another actor.

Sir Lucius O'Trigger has become a symbol of the fire-eating Irishman. He is seriously concerned with fighting. He has a code of honour which drives him on. He wants to marry Delia (whom he supposes to be Lydia) 'with the old gentlewoman's consent' in order to do everything fairly. He is firm with Acres in Act 3 Scene 4, when he hears that he thinks Beverley, as a rival, has supplanted him unfairly with Lydia. Acres, he says, has been provoked; his honour is at stake. He urges Acres to behave in a civil way. He himself wants to meet 'a gay captain' (Absolute) who jested with him 'at the expense of his country' (Ireland) and he intends to call him out for this. His view is that duelling should be undertaken in a polished, polite way. When Lucius finds Absolute in Act 4 Scene 3, and quarrels with him, he is concerned to do so 'genteelly'. In Act 5 Scene 3, at King's Mead Fields, he instructs Bob Acres again, measuring out a short distance 'three or four paces between the mouths of your pistols is as good as a mile'. He realises Acres is a novice at duelling; and chides him when Acres says that he does not feel so bold: 'O fie!—consider your honour'.

He is most disappointed when Beverley does not seem to have arrived. He tells Acres he is not to be trifled with, and criticises him for his valour's oozing away, for being little better than a coward. Then, despising him, he draws his sword in order to fight Jack Absolute. But he is quite ready to make up his quarrel with Absolute: 'Captain, give me your hand—an affront handsomely acknowledged becomes an obligation—'. And when he discovers that Delia is not Lydia but Mrs Malaprop, he takes the trick played upon him with dignity. At the end of the play he hopes no disappointed person is uncontent: he himself is disappointed, but, he says 'it will be very hard' if he has not the satisfaction of seeing other people succeed better'.

Sir Lucius O'Trigger of Blunderbuss Hall comes of a fighting family; he is profoundly serious about duelling—indeed he is practical about it, notably when he asks Acres with all seriousness: 'Would you choose to be pickled and sent home?—or would it be the same to you to be here in the Abbey? I'm told there is very snug lying in the Abbey'. His character is dominated by his love of fighting.

Fag

Fag is Jack Absolute's servant. He is seen as dashing by the coachman ('I doubt, Mr Fag, you havn't changed for the better'), and he is a little affected. He is already tired of Bath when the play opens. He goes to parties with Du Peigne, Faulkland's servant; he is well aware of fashion, and London fashion at that ('Here now—this wig! What the devil do you do with a *wig*, Thomas?—none of the London whips of any degree of *ton* wear *wigs* now').

Fag is on good terms with his master, Captain Absolute. He lies to Sir Anthony Absolute about the reason his son is in Bath. Fag wants to know what line to take for the future ('in order that we may lie a little more consistently'). He informs Captain Absolute that he has not told

Thomas the coachman more than the story about the recruiting mission and supported the lie with details (the recruiting of 'five disbanded chairmen, seven minority waiters and thirteen billiard markers'). He begins by telling Captain Absolute that Thomas is the discreetest of whips, but then emphasises—when Captain Absolute says he hopes Fag has not trusted Thomas—how discreet he has been with him. He asks Absolute to support his lies; he does not object to lying, only to being found out.

He has a wit of his own. After Sir Anthony has had his stormy meeting with his son Fag describes Sir Anthony's manner of leaving in a lively way, giving an impertinent close to his remarks ('upon my credit, sir, were I in your place, and found my father such very bad company, I should certainly drop his acquaintance'.) He reflects upon how the worst temper is shown when one is vexed by someone to revenge oneself upon someone else. Then he himself kicks and beats the errand-boy just as he has been struck earlier by Sir Anthony!

Fag shows concern for his master later in the play (Act 5, Scene 1) when he tells Mrs Malaprop and Lydia about the proposed duel. He speaks in an affected way to Lydia, but he does conduct the ladies to King's Mead Fields to stop the fighting, and he is sensible in sending David to look for Sir Anthony. All in all, this smart servant works well for Captain Absolute, and provides information for the audience at crucial points of the play.

David

In Act 3 Scene 4, David, Bob Acres' servant, a countryman initially, refers happenings at Bath back to Clod Hall, Bob Acres's place in Devonshire. His part in the first scene of the fourth act is amusing, as he utters views on honour (which resemble the famous remarks on honour made by Sir John Falstaff in Shakespeare's *Henry IV*) which are down to earth in their emphasis on the value of life. He sees no point in duelling. He anticipates the way the news of Acres's death will be received at Clod Hall. He gets wildly excited, in Act 5, Scene 1, when telling Lydia about what is going on, and persuading Mrs Malaprop to stop the fighting. This excitement mounts when he finds Sir Anthony in the next scene, blurts out his news about the duel, and says he will call for aid from everyone in authority. He is a warm-hearted man, and clearly fond of his master.

Coachman

The Coachman's function in the play is to convey information in his conversation with Fag in the opening scene.

Mrs Malaprop

The idea of Mrs Malaprop may have been derived from Mrs Tryfort, a
character in *A Journey to Bath*, a play by Frances Sheridan (1724–66),
Sheridan's mother, who was herself a successful authoress. But there are
other possible sources: Mrs Slipslop in the novel *Joseph Andrews* (1742)
by Henry Fielding (1707–54), or Tabitha Bramble in the novel
Humphry Clinker (1771) by Tobias Smollett (1721–71), or Mrs
Heidelberg in *The Clandestine Marriage* (1766), by George Colman
(1732–94) and David Garrick (1717–79).

Mrs Malaprop's name comes from the French *mal à propos*, meaning
'inappropriate'. It suits her nature, for she sometimes uses a word which
resembles the word intended but is completely inappropriate. She also
uses high-sounding words with merely haphazard application. (The
description of Mrs Tryfort given in Frances Sheridan's *A Journey to
Bath* suits her well: 'fondest of hard words, which without miscalling, she
always takes care to misapply').

She is first described, by Fag, as a 'tough old aunt', and in Act 1 Scene
2 she tells Sir Anthony that Lydia wants to disgrace her family and
'lavish herself on a fellow not worth a shilling'. Her actions, in trying to
compel Lydia to forget Beverley, are parallel to Sir Anthony's orders to
Captain Absolute to forget the lady with whom he is in love. Both Mrs
Malaprop and Sir Anthony are ruthless in their attitudes; Mrs Malaprop
agrees with Sir Anthony's proposal of his son, gives 'Mr Acres his
discharge', and will prepare Lydia to receive Jack Absolute's
'invocations'.

Mrs Malaprop is eager to marry Lydia off, because Lydia has learned
of Mrs Malaprop's partiality for Sir Lucius O'Trigger. She welcomes
Captain Absolute when he comes to call; she has learned of Beverley by
bribing Lucy; now she listens to the conversation between Absolute and
Lydia, and interrupts it, getting it all wrong, not realising that Lydia
thinks Absolute is Beverley but pretends he is Captain Absolute. She
continues to be furious with Lydia, who proclaims her love for Beverley.

The classic conflict between youth and age is developed in Act 4 Scene
2 when Sir Anthony brings his son to Mrs Malaprop's lodgings. Here he
urges on Jack to speak to Lydia while Mrs Malaprop urges Lydia to
answer him. Mrs Malaprop is slower on the uptake than Sir Anthony;
when Lydia addresses the Captain as Beverley, she begins to suspect but
is overtaken by Jack's confession. While Sir Anthony likes his imped-
ence and assurance Mrs Malaprop realises it is he who has written the
letter which called her *'an old weather-beaten she-dragon'*. She is,
however, ready, at Sir Anthony's suggestion, to forget and forgive the
lovers.

When she discovers, in Act 5 Scene 1, that the duels are in the offing she is upset that Sir Anthony is not present, as he could prevent 'antistrophe'. She is scornful of Lydia when her niece realises Absolute is involved, and thinks the ladies should not interfere—'it would be very inelegant in us: – we should only participate things'—until she learns that Sir Lucius, too, is involved. Then she is all for rushing to the place of the duels to prevent them, and hustles the others off under Fag's guidance to King's Mead Fields.

In the final scene of Act 5 she, like David earlier, puts honour in its place: 'Come, come, let's have no honour before ladies'. She tells Absolute that Lydia is terrified to death on his account, thus bringing about the reconciliation of the lovers. But because Sir Lucius produces 'Delia's' letter and Lydia denies she is Delia, Mrs Malaprop has to admit she has been writing to him. When he refuses to believe this, she calls him a barbarous Vandyke—and in her last speech says men 'are all barbarians'. She has been gulled, cheated like Malvolio in *Twelfth Night*, a Shakespearean victim of intrigue. But there is hope left, for, in his concluding speech, Sir Anthony says they will drink a health to the young couples 'and a husband to Mrs Malaprop'.

Lydia Languish

Lydia Languish is a creature of romantic sensibility. We know from the conversation of Fag and the Coachman in the opening scene of the play that she is wealthy, but that she is singular enough to prefer Beverley as a half-pay ensign than if she knew he were son and heir to the well-to-do Sir Anthony Absolute. The second scene reinforces this impression that she is romantic, for Lydia is a devotee of romantic novels. And she tells Julia how her aunt has confined her to the house since she intercepted a note and learned of Lydia's connection with Beverley. The correspondence between the lovers had taken an unfortunate turn, for Lydia, afraid that Beverley would never give her an opportunity for a quarrel, wrote an anonymous letter to herself accusing Beverley of paying his addresses to another woman and then showed it to him, saying she would never see him again. And, she tells Julia, the correspondence was intercepted by Mrs Malaprop before she could undo the effect of this teasing. After Julia has left, Lydia stands up for herself against Mrs Malaprop in this scene, and is ordered off to her room. The next time she appears is in Act 3 Scene 3, when Absolute has called on Mrs Malaprop; she thinks he is Beverley pretending to be Absolute and we hear her asking him if he will forgo her wealth. She considers that poverty with him would be charming. When he makes a fine speech to her she thinks she 'could fly with him to the Antipodes'. She is direct with Mrs Malaprop and says no one but Beverley will possess her heart.

Her recognition of Absolute as Beverley in Act 4 seems to solve matters at first, for Jack Absolute is forgiven by his father and Mrs Malaprop. Lydia's romanticism, however, makes her resent Jack's fraud. She thinks he has been treating her as a child, 'humouring' her romance, and, while she thought she was deceiving her relatives, making her in the end the only dupe. She uses her aunt's earlier command—rather as Jack had earlier used his father's demands that he should marry the girl his father had chosen for him—that she should never think of Beverley again, should renounce him, now, for ever. She has been piqued in her pride, but her love for Absolute is genuine as is clear once she hears, in Act 5 Scene 1, that he is involved in the duel, and, subsequently, in Scene 3 she admits her love for him, and finally reminds him that their happiness is unalloyed.

Lydia is a headlong, silly girl, but her silliness and romantic notions, have come from her reading, and her genuine love for Jack Absolute emerges when his life is at risk, and the reality of life replaces the superficial attitudes of sentimentality.

Julia

Julia is a thoroughly unselfish, forgiving girl who is candid and tender. She puts up with Faulkland's nonsensical jealousy and capricious, captious behaviour with patience until, in Act 5 Scene 1, he finally goes too far in pretending that he has commited some crime. But up to then she has managed to put up with his resenting her seeming cheerful in his absence, explaining to him that she had often disguised sorrow (at his unkindness) in similes; she is constant in her affection for him.

He has trifled, she thinks, with her sincerity, and she rightly points out to him what he has lost by doing so. And she keeps from Lydia the cause of her weeping. She even urges Lydia not to tease Absolute, for she herself knows the unhappiness caprice can inflict. But finally she agrees to forgive him, and she makes the final speech in the play, urging them all to study to preserve their happiness, arguing for a realistic state of bliss which will last.

Lucy

Lucy is the pert, scheming maid of comedy *par excellence*. She is clever, as we realise at the end of the second scene in the first act when she reveals how she is extracting money and gifts from Lydia, Captain Absolute, Mrs Malaprop, Mrs Acres and Sir Lucius O'Trigger. We see her in action, getting books from the libraries for Lydia, assuring Mrs Malaprop of her secrecy (she only pretends to be rather silly), giving a letter to Sir Lucius and deceiving him about Delia, telling Fag that Sir

Anthony Absolute has proposed his son as a suitor for Lydia. But having served her purpose in the plot she then disappears.

Plot

The ingredients of the plot are:

(1) the pair of lovers, Jack Absolute and Lydia Languish, apparently kept apart by their elders, Sir Anthony Absolute and Mrs Malaprop. But the older people actually want them to marry once the problem of Beverley/Absolute's identity is cleared up: yet once this is clear Lydia does not want Jack, because she feels he has cheated her. They are reconciled once she realises he is in danger of dying in a duel. The problems have arisen through Jack's deception of Lydia by his pretending to be Beverley.

(2) a second pair of lovers, Faulkland and Julia, kept apart by Faulkland's foibles. He is annoyed that she seems cheerful when they are apart, while he is miserable. He upsets her by taxing her with this; but when she forgives him, he becomes suspicious of her again. When he tests her by pretending he has to flee the country, and she says she will go with him, he tells her he has been pretending; this is too much for her and she does not want anything more to do with him. Yet at King's Mead Fields she manages to forgive him once again, he having realised how stupid he has been. In this relationship deception has again been significant.

(3) another, apparent pair of lovers; 'Delia' is writing to Sir Lucius O'Trigger. He has been led to believe he is corresponding with the niece, not the aunt; but Mrs Malaprop's revelation that it is she who has written to him as Delia ends the matter. In this affair Lucy the maid has been the main agent of the deception.

(4) two quarrels. The first is between Acres and Beverley. Acres is urged by Sir Lucius to issue a challenge to Beverley, which he sends to Beverley by Absolute. When he is finally told, at King's Mead Fields, that Beverley is his friend Absolute, there is no question of a duel. The second is between Sir Lucius O'Trigger and Captain Absolute. Absolute, acting on the tradition that an army officer cannot refuse a challenge, responds to Sir Lucius's challenge though he does not know the reason for Sir Lucius's wish to fight him. It turns out later that he had affronted Sir Lucius unknowingly by making some remarks on Ireland, and when he apologises this duel is also abandoned—though it had got as far as both men drawing swords. Faulkland has been involved as Jack Absolute's second.

(5) the underlying element of the struggle between young and old. Thus Sir Anthony can contemplate cutting off his son and heir if he does not

comply with his wishes. If Mrs Malaprop does not agree to Lydia's marrying before she is of age (twenty-one: but Lydia is seventeen at the time of the play), Lydia can lose most of her fortune. The whole question of marriage was viewed differently in the eighteenth century and earlier. It was normal for marriages to be arranged, and for young people to obey their parents in these matters, particularly where lands, fortunes and families were involved. Parents exercised more power over their children than is usual today.

(6) a contrast between city and country. Mrs Malaprop is vulgar in part because she is trying to live up to an imaginary London standard of behaviour (just as Lydia is trying to live up to, even to out-do the sillier conventions of romance, formed by her decidedly light reading in sentimental romances), and Acres, the country squire, is trying to become sophisticated in urban Bath. In contrast, Jack Absolute and his father have a certain surety of manner that makes their behaviour seem elegant. Sir Lucius O'Trigger, who insists on correctness and polite behaviour, almost despairs of Acres's failure to live up to his standards of how a gentleman should behave.

(7) a contrast between abstract ideas and reality. Faulkland's jealousy, for instance, is unreal, though he is in love; but the nature of that love is firmly criticised by Jack Absolute. Again it is left to David to question the concept of 'honour' underlying the duels. Sheridan who had, after all, his own painful experiences in such matters, is satirising the whole concept of duelling in Sir Lucius's addiction to it.

(8) the element of deception. Fag deceives Sir Anthony; Jack deceives his father and Mrs Malaprop; Lydia deceives her aunt. But deception is most obvious in the case of the lovers: Jack deceives Lydia; she deceives him. Faulkland deceives Julia. Mrs Malaprop deceives Sir Lucius, and Lucy deceives anyone she can!

The plot revolves around the fact that Beverley and Captain Absolute are the same person. Sir Anthony wants his son to marry Lydia Languish, whose aunt also wants this to happen. But Jack Absolute does not at first realise that his father wants him to marry the girl whom he— as the pretended Beverley—is courting; and so the classic conflict between father and son arises. Lydia herself is in love with the supposed Beverley and so resents and rebels against her aunt's trying to compel her to welcome Captain Absolute's advances. There is the added complication that she has quarrelled with him before Mrs Malaprop confined her to the house.

Speech

The dialogue is witty and fast-moving. The characters are sufficiently differentiated. Mrs Malaprop is, of course, the most obvious, her choice of words marking her out as an eccentric. But Bob Acres, in his way of swearing, is equally an original type. Sir Anthony's hectoring, blustering manner is basically that of a hearty extrovert—it turns to a vigorous cheerfulness at the end of the play. There is a differentiation also between the two heroes, for Absolute is lively, polished, polite, whereas Faulkland can be gloomy or sentimentally romantic; and there is a difference, too, between the heroines, for while Lydia is romantic and petulant, Julia is straightforward and pleasant, though she does at times utter various sententious speeches. Fag's conversation is 'smart', whereas the coachman acts as a foil to him. David is rustic and down-to-earth while Lucy the maid affects to be foolish but is actually decidedly sharp and on the make, pert and ready to deceive others in her own interest.

Staging

Sheridan has kept the action in Bath. It takes place in a day. Imagine how you yourself would stage the play. There are eight scenes: a street in Bath; Mrs Malaprop's lodgings, Captain Absolute's lodgings; the North Parade; Julia's dressing-room; Acres' lodgings; the South Parade and King's Mead Fields. There is no need for many 'props'; you will need swords for Sir Lucius, Captain Absolute, Bob Acres and Faulkland and you will need pistols, probably carried in a case, for Sir Lucius and Bob Acres. You will also need letters for Act 2 Scene 2 and Act 3 Scene 3, and books for Act 2 Scene 2, as well as a piece of paper for Lucy's accounts. You will also need a large coat under which Captain Absolute can hide his sword for Act 5 Scene 2. The play, ultimately, depends upon the dialogue and the irony underlying many of its aspects. It is pure comedy, depending upon making fun of unorthodox behaviour as well as exploiting the humour of the situations in which the characters find themselves or have placed themselves. The plot is neat, its reversals of situations are skilfully contrived, and the action moves forward swiftly and surely to its resolution.

Part 4

Hints for study

WHEN YOU READ A PLAY it is worth while remembering that it was written to be performed in a theatre. You will gain from imagining the characters on stage; this will help you to appreciate the way in which the author has constructed the play, how he has worked the action up to various dramatic crises, and how he has provided the tension, the themes that link the various characters together, and the final resolution. A dramatist has to establish the nature of his characters, and you should notice how he does this. Sometimes it is done by idiosyncratic speech. Again, the dialogue provides the interactions of the characters, and you need to consider how it would sound if you heard it spoken by actors and actresses. Indeed the pleasantest way of enjoying a play is to read it aloud, and to enter into the part or parts you are reading, and then, if possible, to see it professionally performed.

In working on a play for an examination it is often a good idea to read the play through quickly to see what happens in it and then to read it again more slowly, making notes as you go, so that you will be able to analyse its construction and appreciate its merits. You will have formed an idea of its nature and the author's purpose in writing it on your first reading. The second reading should help you to understand the play better, and you will naturally be interested in working out the ways in which the author has created his characters, and in seeing how they interact in various situations.

Everyone tends to make different kinds of notes when studying, because people read literature according to their different temperaments. Notes are intended to remind you of different points when you are revising, and making them often clarifies your own thoughts. They can help you to work systematically, and to be able to refer to specific examples when you are discussing aspects of a piece of literature. When you can refer to some action or piece of dialogue in discussing a play your remarks about it will be more effective and persuasive because you will be demonstrating that your ideas are founded on an accurate knowledge of the text you have studied. The kind of notes you might consider making about *The Rivals* could be based on several approaches:

(1) You could consider the play from the point of view of construction. For this you would need to work out what happens in each scene, and to trace how the characters affect each other.

(2) You could consider the play from the point of view of character. Here you might see *The Rivals* as made up of two pairs of lovers who marry and of other would-be lovers who do not succeed in their hopes.

(3) You could consider the play from the point of view of themes. For this you might work out the struggles between the old and the young characters. Or else you could see the play as, partially, a satire upon romantic or sentimental attitudes of mind.

(4) You could consider the play as a representative of one of its kind if you have read enough other comedies to make comparisons.

When you have made your notes it can sometimes be helpful to consider the kind of questions which you may have to answer on the play. The best way to do this is to ask yourself what questions you yourself would set on it. How would you test someone's knowledge of *The Rivals*? How would you frame questions that would encourage a candidate to give his or her reactions to the play? You may find it helpful to have a look at old examination questions: this will familiarise you with the kind of examination paper you will have to answer (some questions are printed in these Notes; see below), and this will enable you to make yourself ready for an examination more sensibly, provided you do not rely on prepared answers, but have made your own notes which help you to answer any kind of question which may be set on the play. In other words, you want to have a clear knowledge of *The Rivals* on which you can draw when you are planning an answer to a question or drafting a plan for an essay.

When sitting an examination, remember to read the examination paper very carefully so that you are certain how many questions you have to answer, and can divide your time efficiently between them. Spend a few minutes planning your answer once you are sure you have chosen the questions which suit you best. Remember in your answers to write an introduction and conclusion, and to give references to the text. Do not tell the story of the play unless you are asked to do so. Do not write down everything you know about the play; answer what you are asked. And leave time to reread what you have written, as you may need to alter something in order to make your answer clearer or more effective.

Questions and specimen answers

(1) What does Fag tell the coachman about Bath in the first scene?
(2) How does Sheridan show us Lydia's romantic nature?
(3) Why has Lydia not made up her quarrel with Beverley?
(4) What role does Lucy play in *The Rivals*?
(5) Write on the character of Bob Acres.

(6) 'Faulkland is a jealous man'. Can you illustrate his jealousy?
(7) In the third act Jack Absolute learns that the wife Sir Anthony intends him to have is Lydia. What complications does this cause?
(8) Julia dismisses Faulkland in the fifth act. Why does she do this?
(9) Write on Mrs Malaprop's misuse of language.
(10) Do you think Sir Lucius O'Trigger contributes vitality to *The Rivals*? If you do, give examples of this.
(11) Write on Jack Absolute's relations with his father.
(12) What functions do the servants perform in the plot of *The Rivals*?
(13) Contrast Jack Absolute and Bob Acres, or Fag and Thomas.
(14) From reading or seeing the play, can you write about life in eighteenth-century Bath?

---

(12) What functions do the servants perform in the plot of The Rivals*?*

In *The Rivals* we have a vestige of the stock servants of classical comedy, who acted as foils to their masters, as messengers and go-betweens in their love affairs, and as confidants as well.

In the opening scene of *The Rivals* the servants are used to give us information about the main characters. Thus we learn that Sir Anthony Absolute has brought Julia Melville to Bath and is gouty (and therefore, bad-tempered), and that Sir Anthony's son, Captain Jack Absolute, is pretending to be Ensign Beverley, because he is in love with the rich Lydia Languish, who is likely to like him better as a half-pay ensign than as heir to Sir Anthony. We also hear of Mrs Malaprop as a 'tough old aunt' and learn that Faulkland is engaged to Julia Melville, and that Jack is bribing Lucy, Lydia's maid. Apart from this information about the main characters (excluding Bob Acres and Sir Lucius O'Trigger), Bath is described from the servants' point of view.

In the second scene of the first act, the conversation between Lucy the maid and Lydia Languish informs us about the fashionable novels read at Bath, provided by the circulating libraries. At the end of the scene Lucy reveals her duplicity. She has been rewarded by Lydia and Ensign Beverley for aiding their plans to elope: but she has betrayed them to Mrs Malaprop, thus bringing about the situation where Lydia is kept at home and cannot make up her quarrel with Beverley. She has had money from Bob Acres for delivering letters (which she never delivered); and she is pretending to Sir Lucius O'Trigger, who also pays her, that the letters from Mrs Malaprop which are signed 'Delia' come from Lydia.

In the opening of the second act we realise that Fag lies to his master, and that he has also lied very efficiently to Captain Jack's father, Sir Anthony, telling him that the captain has come to Bath to recruit. Again, at the end of the first scene of this act, Fag is used to show us how angry Sir Anthony is—and to provide some comedy by himself echoing Sir

Anthony's ill-temper in his own treatment of the messenger-boy.

In the second scene of the second act Lucy tells us that Bob Acres has been 'dismissed'. She gives Sir Lucius a letter and tells him that her mistress talks of him, and when Fag arrives she tells him that Sir Anthony Absolute has proposed his son as a suitor for Lydia. There ensues some comedy, since Fag knows Beverley and Captain Absolute are one and the same. Lucy, who is so devious herself, does not know of Captain Absolute's plot.

In the fourth scene of the third act we see Acres through his servant David's eyes. David thinks his master has changed a great deal by adopting the polish of Bath. In Act 4 David plays a cautionary role, not to say a gloomy one. He tries to put Acres off fighting the duel but in vain.

In the first scene of the fifth act Mrs Malaprop comes in with Fag and David. Fag, in a roundabout way, finally tells Lydia that Captain Absolute is involved in duelling, and David adds to the ladies' fears by his news that Acres and Faulkland are also involved. When he also mentions Sir Lucius O'Trigger Mrs Malaprop is deeply upset. While Fag conducts the ladies to King's Mead Fields, David is sent off to look for Sir Anthony, and in the second scene of this act he comes on stage just after Captain Absolute has got clear of his father. David explains that duelling is about to take place at King's Mead Fields, and offers to call for aid on all the local officers. He supports Sir Anthony (who is suffering from gout) as they rush off to prevent the fighting.

We have had the servants playing a considerable part in explaining the plot and aiding it on its way. They contribute a mixture of town and country manners, David being rustic in speech, and in his attitudes less sophisticated than Fag, while Lucy is very much out for herself—unlike the two menservants who do serve their masters' interests and wish to prevent the duels at the play's end.

---

(14) From reading or seeing the play, can you write about life in eighteenth-century Bath?

Sheridan knew Bath well; he had played his own part in its social life; and that social life provided a suitable framework for his comedy *The Rivals*. In the first scene we have one servant, Thomas the coachman, who has just arrived in Bath, telling Fag, Jack Absolute's servant, that Sir Anthony Absolute has come to Bath because he fears he is about to have another attack of gout. The waters at Bath had long been regarded as medicinal, and that was why so many people went there, to drink the waters at the pump room. Fag tells Thomas that he and his master go to the pump room in the morning, though neither of them drinks the waters. And he also tells Thomas about the rest of the day, spent sauntering on the parades or playing billiards after breakfast. There is dancing at night—but Fag does not like the fact that neither cards nor dancing go on after eleven o'clock at night. The servants are fashionable: they have their own parties, and ape their masters. For instance, wigs are no longer worn.

The second scene shows us how circulating libraries provide light reading, for Lucy the maid has come back to her mistress, Lydia, having tried to get various romantic novels for her, but these have been so much in demand that she has been unable to get them. We learn, too, that some fashionable ladies mark passages in the books they are reading.

Visitors to Bath take lodgings, as we learn from the stage directions to this scene, and visits are paid to friends at these lodgings. Julia Melville, for instance, calls on Lydia Languish, and Sir Anthony Absolute calls on Mrs Malaprop. We learn in the second act about the transport facilities; there are chairmen who carry the sedan chairs. And we realise that it is necessary to dress well in Bath when Bob Acres says he will get rid of his 'hunting-frock' and leather breeches. He has been trimming his hair carefully, too. Later his servant David tells him that he would not be recognised at home.

We find people meeting on the Parades; Lucy, for instance, gives Mrs Malaprop's letter to Sir Lucius O'Trigger on the North Parade, when he has looked in vain for her for half an hour on the South Parade. Sir Lucius meets Captain Absolute on the North Parade later. People take their dancing seriously. Bob Acres rehearses various steps. And we see a further effect of the rules imposed on polite behaviour by the Master of Ceremonies when Absolute replies to Sir Lucius's challenge by suggesting a meeting-place by the Spring Gardens, adding that they will scarcely be interrupted. This reflects the fact that duelling was discouraged (and gentlemen were forbidden to carry swords—'a sword seen in the streets of Bath', says Sir Anthony, 'would raise as great an alarm as a mad dog'), and this is borne out later by Captain Absolute's trying to conceal his sword from his father; and, when his father finds it, by his pretending he is carrying it in order to strike an attitude when he calls on Lydia. We learn, too, that public order is kept, for David tells Sir Anthony he will call on 'the mayor—aldermen—constables—churchwardens—and beadles'. And finally, we see how the facilities of the town are easily and speedily available for parties, for Acres orders 'the fiddles in half an hour to the New Rooms' to celebrate the young couples' having arranged their marriages.

We get some indications of the kind of life lived at Bath from various details in *The Rivals*. It is obviously a compact, homogeneous society where social life has developed its conventions, and elegance and refined behaviour are fashionable, aimed at and appreciated when achieved.

Part 5

Suggestions for further reading

The text

SHERIDAN, RICHARD BRINSLEY: *The Rivals*, included in *The Dramatic Works of Richard Brinsley Sheridan*, ed. C.J.L. Price, Clarendon Press, Oxford, 2 vols, 1973. The definitive edition.

The Rivals, ed. A. Norman Jeffares, English Classics—New Series, Macmillan, London, 1967; St Martin's Press, New York, 1967.

The Rivals, ed. C.J.L. Price, Oxford University Press, London, 1968.

Other works by Sheridan

The Letters of Richard Brinsley Sheridan, ed. Cecil Price, Clarendon Press, Oxford, 3 vols, 1966. The first volume contains Sheridan's letters on *The Rivals*.

Biography and Criticism

MOORE, THOMAS: *Memoirs of the Life of the Right Honourable Richard Brinsley Sheridan*, 1825; 5th edition, 2 vols 1927. The best biography.

BINGHAM, MADELEINE: *Sheridan—The Track of a Comet*, George Allen & Unwin, London, 1972. A lively, modern account of Sheridan's life.

Material on Bath

AUSTEN, JANE: Jane Austen (1775–1817) wrote much in her novels about Bath where she lived for some of her life.

FOOTE, SAMUEL: *The Maid of Bath* (1771). This play satirised life at Bath, the Maid of Bath being Elizabeth Linley, Sheridan's first wife.

GREEN, EMANUEL: *Thomas Linley, R.B. Sheridan and Thomas Mathews: their connections with Bath*, Bath, 1904.

SMOLLETT, TOBIAS: *The Expedition of Humphry Clinker*, 1771; Oxford, 1965. In this novel Smollett gives an account of Bath in the eighteenth century.

The author of these notes

A. NORMAN JEFFARES was educated at Trinity College, Dublin, and Oriel College, Oxford. Before taking up his present post as Professor of English Studies at the University of Stirling he taught classics at Trinity College, Dublin, was Lector in English at the University of Groningen, Lecturer at the University of Edinburgh, Jury Professor of English Language and Literature of the University of Adelaide, and Chairman of the School of English at the University of Leeds. His published work includes a biography of W.B. Yeats and commentaries on Yeats's *Collected Poems* and (with A.S. Knowland) on his *Collected Plays*. He has edited twenty-four plays in *Restoration Drama* (four volumes) and edited work by Congreve, Farquhar, Goldsmith, Sheridan, Cowper, Maria Edgeworth, Whitman and Yeats. His *History of Anglo-Irish Literature* is forthcoming.

York Notes: list of titles

CHINUA ACHEBE
Things Fall Apart

EDWARD ALBEE
Who's Afraid of Virginia Woolf?

MARGARET ATWOOD
The Handmaid's Tale

W. H. AUDEN
Selected Poems

JANE AUSTEN
Emma
Mansfield Park
Northanger Abbey
Persuasion
Pride and Prejudice
Sense and Sensibility

SAMUEL BECKETT
Waiting for Godot

ARNOLD BENNETT
The Card

JOHN BETJEMAN
Selected Poems

WILLIAM BLAKE
Songs of Innocence, Songs of Experience

ROBERT BOLT
A Man For All Seasons

CHARLOTTE BRONTË
Jane Eyre

EMILY BRONTË
Wuthering Heights

BYRON
Selected Poems

GEOFFREY CHAUCER
The Clerk's Tale
The Franklin's Tale
The Knight's Tale
The Merchant's Tale
The Miller's Tale
The Nun's Priest's Tale
The Pardoner's Tale
Prologue to the Canterbury Tales
The Wife of Bath's Tale

SAMUEL TAYLOR COLERIDGE
Selected Poems

JOSEPH CONRAD
Heart of Darkness

DANIEL DEFOE
Moll Flanders
Robinson Crusoe

SHELAGH DELANEY
A Taste of Honey

CHARLES DICKENS
Bleak House
David Copperfield
Great Expectations
Hard Times
Oliver Twist

EMILY DICKINSON
Selected Poems

JOHN DONNE
Selected Poems

DOUGLAS DUNN
Selected Poems

GERALD DURRELL
My Family and Other Animals

GEORGE ELIOT
Middlemarch
The Mill on the Floss
Silas Marner

T. S. ELIOT
Four Quartets
Murder in the Cathedral
Selected Poems
The Waste Land

WILLIAM FAULKNER
The Sound and the Fury

HENRY FIELDING
Joseph Andrews
Tom Jones

F. SCOTT FITZGERALD
The Great Gatsby
Tender is the Night

GUSTAVE FLAUBERT
Madame Bovary

E. M. FORSTER
Howards End
A Passage to India

JOHN FOWLES
The French Lieutenant's Woman

ELIZABETH GASKELL
North and South

WILLIAM GOLDING
Lord of the Flies

GRAHAM GREENE
Brighton Rock
The Heart of the Matter
The Power and the Glory

THOMAS HARDY
Far from the Madding Crowd
Jude the Obscure
The Mayor of Casterbridge
The Return of the Native
Selected Poems
Tess of the D'Urbervilles

L. P. HARTLEY
The Go-Between

NATHANIEL HAWTHORNE
The Scarlet Letter

SEAMUS HEANEY
Selected Poems

ERNEST HEMINGWAY
A Farewell to Arms
The Old Man and the Sea

SUSAN HILL
I'm the King of the Castle

HOMER
The Iliad
The Odyssey

GERARD MANLEY HOPKINS
Selected Poems

TED HUGHES
Selected Poems

ALDOUS HUXLEY
Brave New World

HENRY JAMES
The Portrait of a Lady

BEN JONSON
The Alchemist
Volpone

JAMES JOYCE
Dubliners
A Portrait of the Artist as a Young Man

JOHN KEATS
Selected Poems

PHILIP LARKIN
Selected Poems

D. H. LAWRENCE
The Rainbow
Selected Short Stories
Sons and Lovers
Women in Love

HARPER LEE
To Kill a Mockingbird

LAURIE LEE
Cider with Rosie

CHRISTOPHER MARLOWE
Doctor Faustus

ARTHUR MILLER
The Crucible
Death of a Salesman
A View from the Bridge

JOHN MILTON
Paradise Lost I & II
Paradise Lost IV & IX

SEAN O'CASEY
Juno and the Paycock

GEORGE ORWELL
Animal Farm
Nineteen Eighty-four

JOHN OSBORNE
Look Back in Anger

WILFRED OWEN
Selected Poems

HAROLD PINTER
The Caretaker

SYLVIA PLATH
Selected Works

ALEXANDER POPE
Selected Poems

J. B. PRIESTLEY
An Inspector Calls

WILLIAM SHAKESPEARE
Antony and Cleopatra
As You Like It
Coriolanus
Hamlet
Henry IV Part I
Henry IV Part II
Henry V
Julius Caesar
King Lear
Macbeth
Measure for Measure
The Merchant of Venice
A Midsummer Night's Dream
Much Ado About Nothing
Othello
Richard II
Richard III
Romeo and Juliet
Sonnets
The Taming of the Shrew
The Tempest

Troilus and Cressida
Twelfth Night
The Winter's Tale

GEORGE BERNARD SHAW
Arms and the Man
Pygmalion
Saint Joan

MARY SHELLEY
Frankenstein

PERCY BYSSHE SHELLEY
Selected Poems

RICHARD BRINSLEY SHERIDAN
The Rivals

R. C. SHERRIFF
Journey's End

JOHN STEINBECK
The Grapes of Wrath
Of Mice and Men
The Pearl

TOM STOPPARD
Rosencrantz and Guildenstern are Dead

JONATHAN SWIFT
Gulliver's Travels

JOHN MILLINGTON SYNGE
The Playboy of the Western World

W. M. THACKERAY
Vanity Fair

MARK TWAIN
Huckleberry Finn

VIRGIL
The Aeneid

DEREK WALCOTT
Selected Poems

ALICE WALKER
The Color Purple

JOHN WEBSTER
The Duchess of Malfi

OSCAR WILDE
The Importance of Being Earnest

THORNTON WILDER
Our Town

TENNESSEE WILLIAMS
The Glass Menagerie

VIRGINIA WOOLF
Mrs Dalloway
To the Lighthouse

WILLIAM WORDSWORTH
Selected Poems

W. B. YEATS
Selected Poems